Got Sun?
Go Solar

Got Sun?
Go Solar

Get Free Renewable Energy
to Power Your Grid-Tied Home

Rex A. Ewing *and* Doug Pratt

PixyJack Press LLC

**Got Sun? Go Solar: Get Free Renewable Energy
to Power Your Grid-Tied Home**

Published by PixyJack Press, LLC   PO Box 149, Masonville, CO 80541 USA

FIRST EDITION 2005

9 8 7 6 5 4 3 2 1

ISBN 0-9658098-7-0   (ISBN-13: 978-0-9658098-7-0)

Library of Congress Cataloging-in-Publication Data
        Ewing, Rex A.
          Got sun? go solar : get free renewable energy to power your grid-tied home /
        Rex A. Ewing and Doug Pratt.-- 1st ed.
              p. cm.
          Includes bibliographical references and index.
          ISBN-13: 978-0-9658098-7-0 (pbk.)
          1. Photovoltaic power systems. 2. Solar energy. 3. Wind power. 4. Wind
        turbines. 5. Dwellings--Electric equipment. I. Pratt, Doug. II. Title.
        TK1087.E95 2005
        697'.78--dc22
                                    2005012810

Printed in the U.S.A. on ECF (Elemental Chlorine Free) paper with soy ink.

Distributed to the trade by Johnson Books, Boulder, Colorado.
1-800-258-5830   www.johnsonbooks.com

Book design by LaVonne Ewing.
Back cover photos provided by Bergey Windpower, David Blittersdorf, DC Power Systems,
Evergreen Solar, Global Resource Options, and Real Goods.

To LaVonne Ann,
Forever the sunshine in my soul
- Rex

To my children and
their children's children,
in the hope that mankind will
learn to thrive within its means.
- Doug

Contents

continued

continued

Suppose the chariot of the Sun were given you,
what would you do?

Apollo's question to Phaeton, *Metamorphoses* (Bk II, 74)

Introduction

Have you ever gotten so tired of waiting for someone to do something for you that you finally just did it yourself? That's how most of us learn to fix our bicycles when we're kids: we get fed-up waiting for some disinterested adult—who will probably want an extortionary favor in return—to grudgingly agree to adjust the brakes, or fix a flat tire. Exasperated, you march off to the garage, fish around for a few tools, and get to work on the problem. By the time the repair is done and you're glowing with a self-satisfied sense of accomplishment, you realize it really wasn't all that difficult.

Sound familiar? Then this book is for you; you who have been listening to the chorus singing the praises of solar and wind energy for years, but have seen little more than an ever-bigger national investment in non-renewable energy sources and technology.

But why wait for the "big boys" to bring clean, renewable power to your home at their customary glacial pace when, with a little bit of planning and a few components, you can convert your little piece of earth into an environmentally-responsible haven?

Today's photovoltaic (solar-electric) panels—not to be confused with the huge, heavy hot-water panels that adorned so many roofs back in the 1970s—are cheaper, more efficient and versatile than they've ever been, and modern power inverters can produce an electric current of sufficient power to run virtually any load in any home, while generating an output clean enough to satisfy the persnickety needs of the most delicate electronics.

Got wind? The noisy, awkward, break-down-prone wind turbines of the past have been replaced with quiet, highly-efficient marvels of engineering that can produce useful amounts of power in a gentle breeze.

Many of these new-generation wind turbines can be directly tied into the power grid without the need of batteries or charge controllers.

This is all really cool stuff that wasn't available just a few years ago, and it's just waiting to be installed in, and on, your home.

Do you like the idea of legally spinning your electric meter backwards, and doing it with a simple, non-polluting, silent power source that will outlive your children? That's what solar energy can deliver right now, and this book will explain your options. Solar-electric and wind systems deliver their energy directly to your household, with any surplus pushing out through your meter into the grid. This is called utility intertie, or simply grid-tie, and it's legal in every state.

So what are you waiting for? Whether you're a trained electrician qualified to do the work yourself, or just a homeowner who believes waiting until tomorrow to make the world a better place is not an option, you can use the information in this book to help you decide what type of system will work best for you. Then, with the worksheets in the appendix, you'll be able to size your system to fit your needs. We'll even tell you how to conserve energy in your home to achieve the greatest impact from nature's free and renewable energy sources. By the time you get around to finding an installer, you'll be on intimate terms with your future system.

If you still need a little push, many states offer financial incentives for those willing to invest in solar and wind power, including tax credits and substantial rebates. And should you need financial assistance to get the process kick-started, we'll tell you how to go down that road, too.

Face it: you are all out of excuses. Renewable energy technology is proven, affordable and adaptable to almost any situation, and the financial incentives for investing in solar and wind are about as sweet as they can be.

So, whether you decide to travel down the path to renewable energy on an off-the-shelf Schwinn or a custom-built Madone SSL by Trek, it's going to be your bicycle, so make the best of it. The wait is finally over. ❖

The First Modern Solar Cell

It wasn't exactly serendipity, which is, as they say, looking for a needle in a haystack and finding, instead, the farmer's daughter. No; back in 1952, Daryl Chapin from Bell Labs was definitely looking for the farmer's daughter from the get-go. He just didn't find her in a haystack.

Here's how it happened: Researchers at Bell labs, headed by Chapin, were trying to find a way to operate Bell telephones in remote places, of which there was no dearth back then. Dry cell batteries were short-lived, especially in hot, humid climes, so Chapin was searching for a more satisfactory source of power. Wind was considered, along with thermoelectric power and even steam engines. Chapin, being a solar enthusiast (there was a great deal of interest in passive solar after World War II, due to a worldwide fuel shortage), suggested that the idea of photovoltaics be explored.

At that time, the only PV (solar) cells in existence were made of selenium. Selenium cells, however, could only produce about 5 watts per square meter; a mere 0.5 percent conversion

Crystalline silicon solar cell.

efficiency. Chapin wanted 6.0 percent—a 12-fold increase in efficiency.

As the gods of research would have it play out, two of Chapin's colleagues, Gerald Pearson and Calvin Fuller, were working in a nearby lab with crystalline silicon, in hopes of building a solid-state rectifier, a device that transforms AC to DC. The problem was, pure silicon is a not a very good conductor of electricity. Fuller, however, managed to improve it's conductivity appreciably by introducing the element gallium into the crystal matrix. Then Pearson took it step further: he gave the gallium-rich silicon a bath in hot lithium.

For whatever reason—scientist do so love to play—Pearson shone a light on his crystal and discovered that the light energy induced an electric current. (He certainly must have shouted something like "Eureka!" at that point, though his exact words are lost to history.) It was, in fact, the most efficient solar cell ever created. Pearson rushed to Chapin's office to announce the good news.

Though the first, crude silicon solar cell was not capable of the 6-percent efficiency Chapin was aiming for, it was far better than anything he'd yet found. Chapin went to work to improve it. The big breakthrough came when Fuller vaporized phosphorus onto the surface of a nascent solar cell. This brought the p-n junction (of which you will read more, shortly) near the surface and, perhaps more importantly, allowed for the deposition of conducting channels to carry the light-induced current away from the cell and into an electrical circuit.

By 1954, Chapin, Pearson and Fuller had produced a 6-percent-efficient solar cell and announced it to the world. All that you read in this book follows from their discoveries…

SOURCES: *Solar Today* (Jan/Feb 2004) "Good as Gold: The Silicon Solar Cell Turns 50" by John Perlin, Lawrence Kazmerski, Ph.D., and Susan Moon; and the DOE's Energy Efficiency and Renewable Energy web site, *www.eere.energy.gov/solar/solar_timeline.html.*

ABOVE: The PV-powered space station Skylab. RIGHT: Mars Rover powered by solar panels. *Photos courtesy of NASA and NREL*

In the late 1950s, solar cells were first used in space, and they quickly became the most widely accepted energy source for space applications. In 1964 NASA launches the first Nimbus spacecraft – a satellite powered by a 470-watt PV array. Since then, numerous craft have been launched, including Skylab, and the Mars Rover.

Solar cells are used today to provide power for remote telecommunications, signals and sensors, navigation aids, water pumping, highway call boxes, off-grid lighting, calculators, watches, portable electronics, medical clinics, cathodic protection to prevent iron corrosion, security lighting, billboards, and emergency highway signage...not to mention our homes and offices.

CHAPTER ONE

Why Would You Want A Solar/Wind Electric System?

There are many good reasons to install alternative energy, some of them green, fuzzy, and warm; some of them hard economic facts. Your authors are a cowboy storyteller and a big soft techie so we'll cover the warm fuzzy stuff first.

Warm, Fuzzy Reasons for Renewable Energy

Solar energy isn't diminished by harvesting. The amount of energy we take today in no way diminishes how much we can take tomorrow, or how much is left for our children or grandchildren. Every single day enough solar energy falls on the Earth to supply all the world's energy needs for four to five years. Solar energy shows up directly as sunlight, which is harvested by panels that either create heat, or electricity. Our allotment of solar energy can also show up indirectly as wind, the result of uneven heating on the Earth's surface. Large commercial-scale wind harvesting is a well-developed, rapidly growing industry, and residential-scale wind is seeing some nice advancements. Solar energy also appears as rain. If precipitation falls at higher elevations we can harvest great amounts of energy from falling water—hydro power—another subject that needs it's own book. From our allotment of incoming solar energy, the incredibly tiny fraction of

Everyone's Going Solar

927 megawatts of solar electric modules were installed worldwide in 2004. That's up from 547 megawatts in 2003, and light-years ahead of 21 megawatts in 1983.

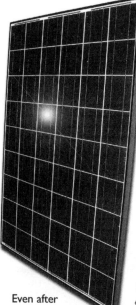

Even after subtracting the CO_2 produced during manufacture and mounting operations, this 187-watt module can be expected to produce enough electricity during the next 30 years to offset the emissions of over 13,600 pounds of CO_2 from utility power. *Photo courtesy of Kyocera Solar.*

a percent that we could potentially harvest will have no effect on world weather. But it can have a dramatic effect on your own well-being, and on the well-being of your offspring, by reducing demands on finite fossil fuel reserves, and by reducing the amount of carbon dioxide (CO_2) that is released to supply your power needs. By supplying some, or all, of our energy needs directly from sunlight we leave more resources for the future, we reduce global warming, and we become better world neighbors.

The kind of panels that turn sunlight into electricity are called photovoltaic modules (say photo-voll-ta-ick), or PV modules for short. PV modules have no moving parts, they are silent and non-polluting. They have manufacturer warranties of 25 years, and useful life spans that will probably exceed 60 years. The embodied energy input required to manufacture them is repaid in two to four years according to studies from the National Renewable Energy Labs. (To read the condensed, two-page report: *www.nrel. gov/docs/fy04osti/35489.pdf.*)

Not that we really need to mention it, but some folks will feel a considerable sense of relief knowing that none of a PV module's raw materials come from the Middle East. Photovoltaic (PV) cells—the dark parts of the module—are made from hi-grade silica, the same raw material as computer chips. It's a primary component of beach sand, although most silica today comes from mining operations, often as a byproduct. The modules use glass covers...more silica, and highly recyclable. The frames of most residential modules are aluminum. That's where all those beer cans go once they've finished their wild youth and they want to do something useful with the rest of their lives. In addition there's a small amount of plastic, used for sealing back covers and junction boxes. Some of it is recycled already; all of it is recyclable in that long-distant future when a PV module has finished its useful life. The mounting structures that support the modules are almost always aluminum with stainless steel hardware.

If there's any part of a modern PV module that started its industrial life under some Mideast sands, it's a tiny fraction of a percent that could just as well come from someplace less volatile. There's a real lack of guilt or exploitation wrapped up with PV modules. If that really bothers you, I suppose you could go rent a Hummer for a weekend to balance your karma.

Hard-Edged Financial Reasons for Solar/Wind Power

You can get a real warm, fuzzy, and highly self-righteous feeling from using renewable energy (RE), but what's it do for your wallet and well-being? A solar/wind electric system allows you to cover part, or all, of your electric needs yourself. Every watt-hour your system delivers is a watt-hour you don't have to buy from your utility company. Once installed and connected to the utility grid, your RE system

A California home with a 3.9 kW solar electric system (21 Sharp 185-watt modules and one Sharp 3,500-watt inverter). *Photo courtesy of Real Goods.*

Calling a Spade, a Spade

Solar panels that make electricity are called "photovoltaic modules" or PV modules for short. This separates them from solar panels that make hot water, which is a very different technology. Water and electricity usually don't mix, and that's certainly true for PV power. We'll be talking about PV modules, or just modules.

A HUGE Array

A 100-mile x 100-mile PV array in Nevada would provide all the electric power for the United States.

will reliably shave your most expensive kilowatt-hours off the top of your bill every month. It offers shelter and protection from rising utility rates in the future. Your solar system is going to last as long as your house, and it's going to reliably crank out watt-hours every day. Your house can have half the electric bill of your neighbors for its entire life! What's that worth? If needed, your solar electric system can be configured to continue providing power to selected circuits during utility blackouts (see chapter 4). This costs a little more, but in storm-battered locales, what are continually-operating furnace, fridge, and lights worth to you?

Many states and utility companies are offering rebates, tax credits, or other incentives for installing solar and wind power. Some of these programs will cover more than 50 percent of the installed cost, which can bring simple payback periods well under ten years. Most folks will see longer payback periods, especially if you assume utility rates won't

Say "Thanks!" to Northern California Pot Growers (and not necessarily for their commercial product)

In the early days of photovoltaics – the 1980s – a curious thing happened. Northern California was overrun with back-to-the-land hippies who'd found cheap, beautiful land and an agreeable climate back in the hills of Sonoma, Mendocino, and Humboldt counties. Much to their surprise however, they found that money didn't grow on trees. But it did grow on bushes! At least on some kinds of bushes. So they did what came naturally, they became growers. This cash crop allowed them to buy groceries, used 4-wheel-drive Toyotas, building materials, and eventually niceties like electric lights. Being miles from the nearest power line, they bought RV lights they could run off a battery. Hauling the battery to town or running the generator to recharge it got old pretty quick, so when the very first solar electric panels started showing up, they embraced the technology wholeheartedly, despite PV costs that were many times more expensive than now. All through the 1980s more than half of the entire U.S. sales of PV modules ended up someplace between Santa Rosa and the Oregon border. It was growers who could afford them, growers who wanted them, and to a very large degree, growers who financed the early development of the PV industry.

rise...uh...yeah right. But every solar electric system will eventually repay its installed cost, probably long before the PV warranty expires, and certainly decades before they wear out. Clean Power Research has developed several software tools that provide highly objective economic analysis of investments in clean energy technologies. Their web-based estimator, with pre-loaded climate, utility rates, and available rebates, is posted by several states with rebate programs, including California, New Jersey, Florida, Ohio, Hawaii, and probably others by the time you read this. Simply do a Google search for "Clean Power Estimator." ❖

Since 1999, the Blittersdorf's *green* home on 10 acres in Vermont has been an excellent example of how renewable energy can be used in the northeastern United States. A 10 kW Bergey wind turbine and 7.0 kW solar array provide all of their electricity, and under a Vermont Public Service Board permit "Certificate of Public Good," they are net metered. The top photo shows a sunroom with PV panels on the roof and the wind turbine. In the lower right corner of the right photo, you can see more of their PV array. Solar hot water panels are also used to heat the swimming pool and home. *Photos by David Blittersdorf.*

Decathlon Marathon

It was time this house finally found a home. As one of 14 entries in the 2002 Solar Decathlon competition, the CU Decathlon house was conceived and constructed by a student group on the University of Colorado campus in Boulder. From there it was disassembled and shipped to the National Mall in Washington D.C. for the contest's 10-part competition, then back to Boulder where it was put up for sale as the competition's overall winner. The buyer was, appropriately enough, Dr. Ronal Larson, Chair-Elect of the American Solar Energy Society (ASES). Ron moved the house to where it now sits, on a panoramic site on Lookout Mountain, west of Golden, Colorado.

In its original design (as mandated by the competition), the house was to be a 650-square-foot off-grid home office, capable of indefinitely maintaining its heating, cooling, lighting and electrical systems without any form of outside energy,

and still have enough energy left over to charge the batteries of an electric car. Ron thinks the house can do exactly that, even though he's currently expanding it to 2,700 square feet before he and his wife, Gretchen, call it home.

The home's 7.2 kW solar array can produce around 30 kWh of electricity on a sunny day, which is far more than needed. The two Outback MX60 charge controllers first top off a bank of 32 L-16 flooded lead-acid batteries, then the dual Xantrex SW5548 inverters send what remains into the electrical grid (a more worthwhile undertaking than in previous years, now that Colorado allows net metering and time-of-day rates). Heat for the hydronic in-floor heating system is gathered year-round with the original array of evacuated solar-collection tubes and four add-on standard hot water panels working together to heat 10,000 gallons of water stored in two insulated concrete tanks along the north wall of the walkout lower level. A pair of secondary-combustion wood stoves serve as backup during winter months.

What remains? A plug-in hybrid car he and Gretchen can employ to exercise the home's beefy battery bank.

The 2002 Solar Decathlon winner (top) is now part of Larson's home (left). For more information about this university-level competition: http://solar.colorado.edu.
Left photo by LaVonne Ewing.

CHAPTER TWO
Is This Stuff Legal...or Safe?

Way back in 1978, mostly as a result of the '73 Arab oil embargo, and to encourage renewable energy development, the Federal government passed the Public Utilities Regulatory Policies Act (PURPA) which says that any private renewable energy producer in the USA has the right to sell excess renewable energy to their local utility company. Until PURPA, only large-scale mills and factories were able to sell excess energy back to the grid. Now the door was open to everyone. The federal law didn't say that utilities had to make this easy, or profitable, however. And believe me, it wasn't/isn't either. Interconnection standards were whatever your local utility said they were, which made it nearly impossible for small-scale wind and solar manufacturers to develop and mass-produce standardized equipment. And without standards, the utilities justifiably worried about safety. Would this customer's equipment shut off automatically if utility power went off? Demands for the customer to carry million-dollar liability insurance were not uncommon. Payment wasn't anything to get excited about either. Under PURPA rules, the utility has to pay their "avoided cost," which is usually defined as their wholesale rates, but can get sticky because wholesale rates vary widely depending on time of day and

PV: A Growth Industry

Solar energy demand has grown at about 25% per year over the past 15 years. Conventional utility grid energy demand typically grows 0 - 2% per year.

season. Usually it works out to around two to four cents per kilowatt-hour. None of this was the least bit encouraging, and renewable energy development in the U.S. languished throughout the '80s.

A home on Long Island, New York with a 2.7 kW array of Evergreen solar modules. *Photo courtesy of Evergreen Solar.*

Net Metering

In the mid '90s individual states started passing "net metering" laws which allowed small-scale producers to very simply sell excess renewable energy to the utility through their existing meter for standard retail rates. This means you could push a kilowatt-hour of energy into the grid during a sunny afternoon, buy a kilowatt-hour back later that evening, and enjoy a total of zero on your meter. This sure beats selling it for two cents, then buying it back for ten cents. Net metering laws are a very good deal for renewable energy producers because it allows us to treat the utility like a big, never-full, never-wears-out, 100 percent-efficient battery, that we don't have to buy, service, or maintain. It isn't such a great deal for utilities, who get to buy your kilowatt-hour for ten cents, then sell it to your neighbor for ten cents. For this reason, most utilities have negotiated caps on how much net-metered power they're required to purchase, usually expressed as a percentage of their total and how long a customer can hang onto a credit. As of early 2005, there is not a blanket Federal net metering law, but thirty-three states have state-wide laws, and an additional six individual utilities actively support net metering. To see how net metering is becoming the norm, and to check out your state, see *www.dsireusa.org.*

What if you're not in a net metering state? All is not lost, but first contact your state representatives and ask why not...why is your state in the minority? Get on the ball! Then contact your friendly local electric utility and ask what their policy is with small-scale renewable energy producers. We've heard stories from customers about small utility companies that, when faced with the choice of developing a unique billing system for a single customer, or even a handful of them, simply take the easy way out and allow net metering. If that doesn't fly, you might consider a smaller system that doesn't sell back much. Remember that every electron your solar/wind electric system delivers, is one electron you don't have to buy. You're getting the same one-to-one effect as net metering, up until your production starts to exceed your household use.

Do I Need a Special Electric Meter?

In most cases the answer is no, but it's probably going to be a different meter than the one you've got now. The common mechanical clockwork meters will run forward or backward just fine. They aren't, however, calibrated to record accurately in reverse. So your utility should provide a calibrated bi-directional meter. Utilities usually provide single-rate, bi-directional meters at little or no charge...after all, it's their meter. If you're on a time-of-use billing scheme, then you'll need a very special meter, and that may have a one-time installation charge.

Occasionally a ratchet is installed on a meter so it can only run in one direction. This is often how differential buying and selling rates are handled. Two meters are installed in series.

One will only read input, the other will only read output.

The new digital meters are another story. Many of the fully digital meters simply have a little magnet on the wheel. It counts one revolution every time the magnet goes by, assuming that it only goes by in the forward direction. You could be paying for every kilowatt-hour you send out! I actually caught my helpful utility company installing a meter like this (twice!), when they thought they were installing a bi-directional meter. It had a "bi-directional" sticker inside, but it didn't register bi-directionally, and managed to get on two different service trucks on two different days. So always check – you want to see that baby registering backwards!

– Doug Pratt

Rebates and Incentives

A great resource for the latest information on rebates and incentives is the **Database of State Incentives for Renewable Energy** at **www.dsireusa.org**. Just click on your state for a complete listing of rebates, incentives, tax breaks, or any other way that money is available for clean energy in your state.

Why Your Utility Company Doesn't Want Your Power

Utility companies are naturally going to be very concerned about any source that could be feeding energy into their network. Is the frequency, voltage, and waveform within acceptable limits? The utility is going to accept your power only if it's as good or better than the product they normally deliver. Is it clean enough to sell to the neighbors? The utility is responsible for any power quality problems once they accept your solar-generated electrons. What happens if the utility power fails? Line workers could be at risk if your system continued feeding power to the grid after a failure. There are many highly valid reasons for utility companies to be less than enthusiastic about accepting power input from small independent producers. Once it's in their system, they bear total responsibility if something happens to the neighbor's TV due to power quality problems.

Technology Leads...

Trace Engineering started producing their intertie-capable SW-series inverters in about 1994—95. This was the first really affordable intertie inverter. It brought the possibility of utility intertie within reach for everyday folks. And it was so easy! Just connect your PV modules to your batteries like usual, connect your batteries to your inverter like usual, and connect your inverter AC1 terminals to utility power, unlike the usual. (The AC2 terminals went to the usual generator.) Folks started hooking them up to utilities and pushing the "sell" button almost immediately...sometimes with official approval, but often without it. It worked fine either way. Funny how software doesn't care about legalities.

Meanwhile, various states were passing laws that said if their citizens wanted to sell excess renewable energy back to the grid, the utility had to accept it. And in many cases, they had to accept it via net metering, which gave retail rate credits to the homeowner. Utilities were scrambling. On the one hand, state law said they had to accept this power, on the other hand, they had no idea how clean, safe, or regulated this power was. There were several years where utilities, in order to protect themselves, had to go buy examples of grid-tie (intertie) inverters, set them up, and test them for themselves. PG&E of California, the nation's largest utility company, had a list of accepted inverter models. A very short list. So long as you installed something on their list, you could get approved for net-metering intertie. Many smaller utility companies either stonewalled, because they couldn't or wouldn't deal with the confusion, or simply accepted anything on PG&E's list.

A very large residential array that averages about 50 kWh per day (Yeeowseers!) *Photo courtesy of Shell Solar.*

...And Regulations Follow

Meanwhile, in the background, standards and regulations were being developed as quickly as possible. UL standard 1741 was first unveiled in May 1999 to address "distributed generation," a new class of electrical equipment that can potentially push power back into the grid. Here was the small-scale interconnection standard we needed, but never had, all through the 1980s and 1990s. The UL1741 interconnection standards have already been updated and expanded several times, as is normal for new standards. It sets precise limits for how low or high the voltage can wander, how much distortion is allowed in the waveform, what has to happen under any conceivable utility condition, and how fast it all has to happen. As it has been updated, UL1741 has been incorporating industry standards for distributed generation power delivery as they've been developed. In addition to UL1741 compliance, some inverter manufacturers will list a series of IEEE (Institute of Electrical and Electronics Engineers) standards. IEEE 519, which defines power quality standards, and IEEE 929 which defines anti-islanding, are the most common. The end result is that the output power from a grid-tie inverter is held to much higher standards than your local utility has to meet. UL1741 guarantees better-quality power to the homeowner than your local utility can promise. All grid-tie inverters on the market are now certified to this standard, which means they have been rigorously (expen$ively!) tested and proven to deliver cleaner, tighter, better regulated power under all conditions. If your utility power fails, or the power quality wanders

Turning On Northern California's First Residential Grid-Tie System

Back in late 1995, I had the dubious pleasure of punching the "sell" button on what was apparently PG&E's first residential solar electric intertie system with net metering. At least it was the first one that PG&E knew about, and the pleasure was dubious because…well, let me tell you the story.

In '92 and '93 I had designed and consulted on the installation of a nice hybrid solar electric/wind system at the north end of the Napa Valley. Even though the customer (we'll call him George) was right next to the county road with readily-accessible power lines, he chose to build his passive solar house off-grid. This was intended as George's retirement home, and no power bill would be one less future uncertainty. But retirement was several years away yet, so for tax purposes he made it a rental property in the meanwhile.

For the most part this worked out fine, except for a few times in the depths of winter when there was no sun for two or three weeks. Neither the tenants nor George liked dealing with generators. So when the State of California announced that as of January 1995 small grid-tie systems would be legal, George was first in line with his application. This was a strange new critter to PG&E, and they took their time granting approval. In the meantime we did a little equipment upgrading, and George was ready by March. It was late September when the local electrician finally called to tell me George had been approved for turn-on in early October. And, oh, by the way, a couple PG&E bigwigs wanted to be there when we officially punched the sell button. Would I mind being on hand to answer any questions? No problem. The site was an hour and a half of very scenic twisty roads from my work. It was a great ride on my beemer.

So on the appointed day I showed up, dressed in what I thought was appropriate garb

outside the standards, the inverter will stop selling power within a maximum of 75 milliseconds. Most utilities agree this is probably quicker than their repair crews on most days.

Even exceedingly unlikely scenarios are anticipated, like islanding. A utility island happens (theoretically) when the utility power fails, but leaves a small isolated area like you and a few neighbors who happen to be using precisely as much energy as your grid-tie system is delivering at the moment. So long as everything stays in balance (a highly improbable assumption) such an island could keep running for a long time, except that some over-caffeinated official already thought of it. So every couple minutes the inverter will do a little hiccup as an island check. The point is, UL1741 is exhaustively thorough. Every possible problem, and even a few impossible ones, have been considered, and if necessary, a performance standard has been written to protect all involved.

(red and black motorcyle leathers). Much to my surprise, PG&E had brought an entire bus! And it was mostly full of engineers, each of whom had at least twenty urgent questions! I was quickly surrounded and barraged. Now I know how celebrities feel. Fortunately for me, I'd packed several extra copies of the copious Trace SW-Series Owner's Manual. I tossed these out to the crowd. It was like tossing raw meat to a pack of wolves; they all went off to corners to devour the goodies. I knew from talking to the Trace folks that PG&E had been testing several of these inverters in their labs someplace for over six months. I guess their engineers are fairly spread out and don't get to talk with each other as much as they should.

The time came to activate George's system.

I went into the power room, while most of the PG&E crew went outside to watch the meter. I punched the "sell" button, enabling the inverter to start selling excess PV power. Outside, as the meter dial slowed, stopped, and then started rotating backwards I could hear everyone go, "ooooohh!" After all, nobody had ever seen this before. This was quickly followed by shouts of, "Oh! Oh! Do it again! Do it again!" So we simulated a couple of PG&E power failures and demonstrated how it wouldn't sell if it couldn't sense utility power. This made everyone a lot more comfortable, and everybody went home pleased with the day.

– Doug Pratt

Is it Grid-tie or Intertie?

Two new words have appeared to describe this new practice of treating the utility grid like a big battery. We've used both terms interchangeably, because they are. *Intertie* is probably more descriptive of the give-and-take relationship, but *grid-tie* will be understood by more folks. Once you own one, you can call it whatever you want.

Having a precisely-written UL performance standard assures both utilities and customers that these inverters simply cannot present any threats to workers or owners. It has also helped to curb most of the absurd insurance demands that some utility companies were attempting to impose on customers, such as million-dollar liability coverage. Most utilities have backed off, and several states have specifically outlawed any additional requirements for interconnection, so long as all components are UL listed. For several years this left an amusing artifact clause in the PG&E interconnection agreement, where an grid-tie customer was "...required to maintain no less liability insurance than they currently carry." Uh...sure. We can do that.

In addition to UL specifications, we're starting to see equipment with FCC (Federal Communications Commission) compliance ratings. An FCC rating isn't mandatory...yet, but it probably will be in a few years, and most manufacturers are voluntarily complying, especially as they develop new designs. The FCC Part 15, class B rating you're likely to find on your inverter says that this appliance will cause minimal interference with radios, TVs, and other common wireless devices. Note we said minimal, rather than no interference. Inverters all make some electronic noise. If you're close enough, with the right gizmo, you're still likely to get some interference. But your chances of being able to listen to the ball game on AM radio are greatly improved with this new generation of FCC compliant inverters. ❖

United States 9%

Rest of Europe 8%

Rest of World 14%

Germany 39%

Japan 30%

Source: Solarbuzz Inc.

World 2004 PV Market Installations
(Share of Megawatts)

CHAPTER THREE

Riding Herd on Electrons: Electricity and Solar Cell Basics

Now that you are acquainted with the legalities of grid-tied solar and wind systems, it's time to get down to the *really* fun stuff...like, how does it all work?

Electrons Have All the Fun

When you're talking about things electrical, you are really talking about electrons and their highly predictable tendencies. Electrons, for those of you who have successfully managed to repress all memories of chemistry class, are the negatively-charged particles that orbit atomic nuclei at breakneck speeds from comparatively great distances. They are unimaginably tiny things; so tiny, in fact, that it would take 166,000,000,000,000 of them laid out like beads on a string to span the period at the end of this sentence. Just the same, as diminutive as they may be, electrons hold everything together, since all molecules are collections of atoms eager to share each others electrons.

"Big deal," you say. "What's all this got to do with solar energy?" I was just getting to that.

When electrons aren't holding stuff together, they are usually involved in making electricity. Plug in a vacuum cleaner, turn on a radio, or stick a slice of bread in a toaster, and all you're really doing

Not Everyone Can Flip A Switch

Two billion people in the world have no access to electricity. For most of them, solar photovoltaics would be their cheapest electricity.

Source: SolarBuzz.com

is opening the floodgates to permit a multitude of electrons to flow from a place where they reside in abundance, to a place where there is a dearth of the evasive little things.

It's not a free ride, of course. We fully expect to get paid for our efforts. How do we collect? By putting obstacles in the electrons' path. Obstacles such as electric motors, induction coils, or heating elements. If electrons want to get from here to there—and they really, really do—they're going to have to do some work along the way. It's only fair; we just can't let them have all the fun.

Learning To Love Volts, Amps and Watts (but not ohms)

Voltage is a measure of electrical potential.

Amperage is a measure of the total amount of electricity that passes a given point over a given amount of time.

Wattage is simply a measure of the amount of electrical power provided by the circuit.

Electricity, then, is simply the flow of electrons through a conductor from one place to another. Gazillions of them. And, if you hope to do some of your own system planning, there are exactly three terms you will need to acquaint yourself with: voltage (volts), amperage (amps), and wattage (watts).

Voltage is a measure of electrical potential. In electrical terminology, voltage is called the "electromotive force" of an electrical circuit. Though it's a shameful act of anthropomorphism, you could think of electrical potential as the desire a pack of electrons has to get from one place to another. The greater the desire, the higher the voltage. This is why a spark from the end of a spark plug wire will jump an inch or more to an engine block. At 30,000 volts, the electrons are highly motivated to get out of the wire and into the metal block to complete the circuit (though, if your hand is carelessly close to the end of the wire, the electrons will consider it a conductor, too).

Amperage, by contrast, is a measure of the total amount of electricity that passes a given point over a given amount of time. The rate of flow, in other words. Technically, an ampere is one volt of electricity passing through one ohm of resistance. (What's an ohm? It's a measure of resistance to the flow of electricity, and it will not figure into any of your calculations, unless you choose to go about them the hard way.)

That leaves wattage, which is simply a measure of the amount of electrical power provided by the circuit. A watt is defined as the amount of work done when one ampere at one volt flows through one ohm of resistance. (Really—you don't have to worry about ohms.) It is equal to 1/746th of a horsepower.

Putting these terms together, we learn that:

Volts x Amps = Watts

So, if your circular saw draws 5 amps of power when plugged into a 120-volt wall outlet, it will consume 5 x 120 = 600 watts of power. By reworking the equation, we can see that:

Watts ÷ Amps = Volts   and   **Watts ÷ Volts = Amps**

Together, these three equations will likely be the basis for every bit of number crunching you'll need to do when designing and operating your system.

Falling Water and Electron Flow: A (Nearly) Perfect Analogy

If you're still a little confused about the relationship between volts, amps and watts, you are probably not alone. Fortunately, a little analogy should help bring things into focus.

Imagine that you have two tanks of water. One is 20 feet overhead, the other twice that high. Both have hoses of equal diameter attached to the outlets. Opening the nozzles on both hoses, you will notice that the hose attached to the loftier of the two tanks produces twice the flow of the other. That's because the water in the 40-foot

Rex's Raillery

One ampere at one volt is equal to 6,250,000,000,000,000,000 electrons passing a given point in one second. Running a 60-watt bulb for one minute requires the services of 22.5 sextillion (2.25×10^{22}) electrons. This figure exceeds the number of special-interest lobbyists in Washington, D.C. – at least for the time being.

Electricity's Who's Who

The **volt** is named after Count Alessandro Giuseppe Antonio Anastasio Volta, the Italian-born physicist who invented the electric battery in 1800.

The **ampere** gets its name from André-Marie Ampère, a French contemporary of Volta who was the first to combine the phenomena of electricity and magnetism into a single electromagnetic therory.

tank has twice the kinetic potential of the 20-foot tank. This kinetic potential of water is analogous to that in the electrical potential—the voltage—of an electrical circuit.

What about the amperage? If amperage is a measure of the rate of flow, and the water from one tank is flowing out at twice the rate as water from the other, isn't that twice the amperage? No, it's the same. This is because volts and amps are defined by each other—when you talk about amps you are really talking about volt/amps. Amperage is the rate of flow at a given voltage. So, you can raise one of the water tanks higher and higher, thus steadily increasing the pressure, but you still will not increase the rate of flow (amperage) as it relates to water falling from a given height (voltage).

In fact, the only safe way to raise the amperage in our water analogy is to increase the size of the hose. That's why thick wires can carry more current than thin ones. Of course, you could attach a pump to the end of the hose and pull water out of the tank at a faster rate than the hose was meant to handle. This would be analogous to running power to a 30-amp, 240-volt welder with a skimpy lamp cord. Not a good idea.

This leaves us with wattage, the amount of work being done. To illustrate what wattage really is, we'll attach turbines to the ends of both hoses. As you might imagine, water flowing from the 40-foot tank will turn the turbine twice as fast as water from the 20-foot tank, thereby performing twice the work. How do we get an equal amount of work from the water in the 20-foot tank? You guessed it— we double the carrying capacity of the hose. This is akin to doubling the amperage, and will give us the same wattage (amount of work done) as the smaller hose attached to the higher tank:

A 40-foot drop x 1 unit of carrying capacity =
a 20-foot drop x 2 units of carrying capacity
or: 40 volts x 1 amp = 20 volts x 2 amps

Isn't this simple? Don't get too complacent, however, because now I'm going to throw a little wrinkle into our nice, smooth analogy. It has to do with the inherent differences between rubber hoses and copper wires. For, whereas a rubber hose will eventually burst when subjected to enough pressure (voltage), a copper wire will suffer no such ill effects. The 30,000 volts coursing through a skinny spark-plug wire is a case in point. Because the amperage is negligible, the small wire can handle the current, even though the voltage is immensely higher than anything you would ever use in your home.

This non-intuitive fact leads to a practical conclusion: if you increase the voltage of your solar array, you will be able to use smaller wire to conduct the current to the house. In fact, by doubling the array voltage—from, say, 24 to 48 volts—you are quadrupling the carrying capacity of the wire. How? Let's say you have a solar array capable of producing 960 watts of power. If your system is 24 volts, you will need wire sized to carry 40 amps of current ($960 \div 24 = 40$). If you increase your array voltage to 48 volts, however, your wire only needs to be sized to carry 20 amps ($960 \div 48 = 20$). And, in addition to halving your amperage, you are also halving the percentage of the voltage lost due to resistance in the wire, hence you are increasing the wire's carrying capacity four-fold.

Confusing? Let's take a real-life example. We'll say that your 960-watt array is 90 feet from your house. By referring to the Wire Size/Line Loss tables in the appendix, you will see that with a 48-volt array, you can use #4 wire (just .204 inches in diameter) to span 90 feet with an acceptable 2 percent line loss (the amount of voltage lost to resistance within the wire). But if your array were 24 volts, the #4 wire would only carry the current for 22.5 feet at 2 percent line loss. To span the full 90 feet, you'd need to use a 3/0 wire. This is essentially heavy welding cable .410 inches in diameter and four times heavier (and pricier) than the #4 wire.

Repeat after me: Voltage is Good.

Electricity's Who's Who

The **watt**, on the other hand, is named after Scottish-born inventor, James Watt, whose passion was not electricity, but steam engines. Though he didn't dabble in electron flow, he did introduce the term "horsepower," and in 1889, 76 years after Watt's death, the Second Congress of the British Association for the Advancement of Science adopted the watt — equal to 1/746th of a horsepower — as the unit of electrical power.

AC/DC: It's More Than Rock 'n Roll

Throughout the 1880s, Thomas Edison and George Westinghouse waged a private war to determine whether the electric lights in New York City (and eventually everywhere else) would be powered with direct current (DC), or alternating current (AC). Edison argued that the inherent danger of electrocution made AC too deadly for general use, while Westinghouse countered that DC could only be transmitted a short distance without resorting to the use of prohibitively

Series vs. Parallel

There are two ways to wire a solar array or a battery bank, and in all probability you will employ them both. In a series circuit, the electrons are given but a single path to follow. As you add solar panels (or batteries), therefore, the electrical pressure (the voltage, in other words) within the wires is increased, but the amperage remains unchanged. So, to create a 48-volt circuit with two 24-volt solar panels, you would link them together like beads on a string, connecting the positive terminal on the first panel to the negative terminal on the second panel to achieve the required voltage, while leaving the amperage unchanged. But what if you have four 24-volt solar panels in a 48-volt array? You would create a pair of series strings of two panels each, then connect the two strings in parallel, joining positive to positive, and negative to negative. This provides more than one path for the electrons to follow, so the voltage remains the same while the amperage is doubled.

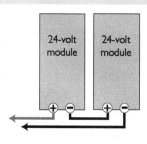

Two modules wired in **SERIES**
for 48 volts

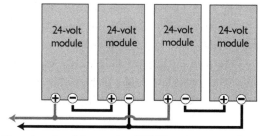

Two pairs of modules wired in **SERIES** and then in **PARALLEL**
for 48 volts

heavy wires. The issue was finally resolved in 1891 when Edison's firm merged with AC arc-light producer, Thomas-Houston. The new company came be known as AC appliance giant General Electric. Edison, who had no control over the new company, never admitted defeat. He simply claimed he had more important things to do than waste his time on electric lighting.

Today, we're still using alternating current for most of our electrical needs, and primarily for the reasons George Westinghouse espoused over a century ago. But what is AC, exactly, and how does it differ from DC?

DC is simplicity, itself. It is merely a steady stream of electrons traveling along a conductor from one place to another. It is the current that powers all the systems in an automobile, and the current that flows from a photovoltaic module (solar panel) to a battery or inverter. It is the only form of electricity that can be stored in a battery.

AC is bit more complicated. Graphically, it can be pictured as a graceful wave (called a sine, or sinusoidal, wave) that undulates from a positive peak to a negative trough, and back again. Essentially, it is an electrical current that reverses its direction of flow several times per second (60 cycles per second, or hertz, in the USA, 50 hertz in most of Europe).

If you live in a house that is powered (all, or in part) by a solar array, you will be employing both DC and AC, and a large chunk of the money you'll spend will be for the inverter, a mysterious component that converts the DC from the solar array into the AC needed by your house. If your system includes batteries, the inverter will be located between the batteries and the AC sub-panel used to power critical systems. Otherwise, your solar array will connect directly to the inverter.

Either way, both types of current are necessary for your solar-powered home. So, in addition to doing your part to clean up the

Break a Deal, Face the Wheel (or the AC generator)

Nikola Tesla almost single-handedly invented AC power. Yet Tesla's first employer in America was, ironically, Mr. DC himself, Thomas Edison. When Edison stiffed Tesla on a $50,000 bonus he had promised, Tesla walked out without a word, eventually finding his way to Westinghouse's door.

environment and save the world, you're vindicating Thomas Edison in a way the clever old inventor could never have imagined. I don't know about you, but it sure makes me feel good.

But why was Westinghouse able to send his AC farther than Edison could send his DC? It all relates to a principle called inductance, and the work done by Croatian immigrant and Westinghouse employee, Nikola Tesla. What is inductance? It's the spooky property of an electrical current to create an electromagnetic field around a wire whenever the strength of the current changes. With DC it doesn't really

A Look Inside an Inverter

The heart of an inverter is the transformer. It takes low-voltage DC from the batteries or solar array and turns it into the high-voltage AC we use to power our homes. Transformers, however, work on the principle of inductance, a phenomenon that only occurs to any significant degree in the presence of a pulsing (alternating) current. It takes some clever trickery to convince the transformer the direct current driving it is AC.

The magic behind the deception is a configuration called an H-Bridge. Each of the two legs of the H have a transistor switch near each end—four switches in all—and the legs are joined by the transformer in the middle. The two bottom switches control the flow of the negative current from the DC source, while the upper switches control positive flow back to it. By electronically timing the opening and closing of the switches, the current can be made to flow first one way, then the other, through the transformer. Voilà—alternating current!

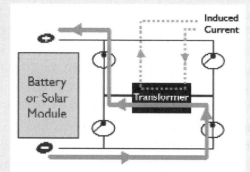

By rapidly opening and closing switches on opposing corners, current flow is reversed and an alternating current is induced in the transformer.

matter a whit, since the only time the current varies is when it's turned on or off. But with AC, the current is continuously changing strength and direction, so it's forever sending pulses of electromagnetic waves coursing back and forth along the wires.

As it turns out, these pulses of electromagnetic radiation can be picked up by nearby wires, and a current can be induced inside them, even if no current is flowing directly through the wire. If, for instance, a coil of wire (let's call it the secondary coil) is wound around another coil (the primary coil), a current will flow in both coils, once

electricity is sent through the primary coil. Moreover—and this is the really important part—if the secondary coil contains twice as many turns in its windings as the primary, the current induced in the secondary coil will be at twice the voltage. Likewise, if the secondary coil has half as many turns, the voltage will be reduced accordingly.

Thanks to the work done by Tesla to perfect the transformer, Westinghouse could begin with a very high voltage at the generating station, and step it down along the way until it became 120-volt house current. Edison, by contrast, had no way to manipulate DC and therefore had to run extremely heavy wires to facilitate the movement of low-voltage DC.

Useful things, those transformers, and they owe all their utility to the principle of inductance.

Inductance does have a downside, however, since it's the reason you can electrocute yourself relatively easily with AC, and it's practically impossible with DC—it's those electromagnetic waves that getcha. So, next time you get shocked, blame it on Nikola Tesla and George Westinghouse.

A pole barn in upstate New York is used as a grid-tied 10kW power station for a farmhouse located about 150 feet away. The 64 Kyocera KC158 solar modules serve as a functional roof for the storage barn, and four SMA Sunny Boy 2500 inverters and remote control are located at the farmhouse. *Photo courtesy of Triangle Electrical Systems, Plattsburg, New York.*

Solar Cells: Teaching Old Electrons New Tricks

The heart of any solar-electric system is, appropriately enough, the photovoltaic module, commonly known as the solar panel. A solar panel is usually the squarish unit you buy and mount next to other squarish panels in a solar array, but it can also be in the form of a roof shingle, or even a standing-seam roof panel. Whatever form it's in, commercial panels are typically made of single-crystalline silicon, polycrystalline silicon, or even non-crystalline (usually called thin-film or amorphous) silicon. Any way you cut it, slice it or dice it, it comes out silicon.

A solar panel is not the basic unit, however. All solar panels are made up of a number of solar cells, each producing around 0.5 volts of electrical potential. Within the matrix of the panel, these cells are connected in series to achieve the desired voltage, usually in the range of 16 – 17, or 32 – 34 volts.

Keeping this in mind, we can now answer the one question burning so hot in your mind right now, namely: how do solar cells turn sunlight into electricity? Let me indulge you.

What's So Great About Silicon, Anyway?

Largely because of the ubiquity of computers, anyone who has not been living in a cave for the past two decades knows that silicon is a semiconductor of electricity—it sort of allows an electrical current to pass through it, but hardly with the facility of copper or aluminum. Oddly enough, it's this quasi-standoffish attitude of silicon that makes it so useful in the manufacture of solar cells.

Chemically, silicon has 14 positively-charged protons, and 14 negatively-charged electrons. This would seem to be a happy arrangement, if not for the fact that it has room for four more electrons in

Doug's Detour

Solar energy depends on nuclear power! It's true. PV modules are just long-distance antennas for nuclear energy. The power plant, however, is a relatively safe 90 million miles away. It's called the Sun.

its outer energy level. How does it get them? It could snatch four passing electrons from somewhere, but there would be no protons to hold them in place, so the kidnapped electrons would soon escape. So instead, it borrows them from other silicon atoms, forming a crystal lattice in the process (except in the case of amorphous silicon). In this crystal, every atom of silicon is attached to four other atoms of silicon and they all share electrons. In other words, every silicon atom has the four extra electrons it wants, with no net charge, since the protons in the crystal exactly balance out the electrons. It's a really cushy setup.

Silicon Doping: Homogeneity's Undoing

In fact, it's far too cushy for our purposes. Happy silicon with happy electrons is pretty useless if we want it to do any work. We need to stir things up a bit. How? By adding impurities to it. Say, a few atoms of phosphorus. Phosphorus has five electrons in its outer energy level, so if it is introduced into the silicon crystal lattice (in a process called doping), that fifth electron will be frantically looking for a place to fit in. Now we have an unhappy electron, and that makes us happy.

But we're just getting started. A melancholy electron wandering aimlessly in search of a home doesn't do us much good. We need to give this electron a purpose—something it can aspire to. We do this by making another silicon crystal, this time doping it with a different impurity, say boron. Having only three electrons in its outer energy level, a boron-doped silicon crystal will have empty spaces where electrons could be, but aren't. These empty spaces are called holes, and each of these holes would like to have an electron to call its own.

Are you beginning to see where this is leading?

Our phosphorus-doped silicon is called n-type, in honor of the

Over its lifetime, this single 175-watt module should produce 12,000 kilowatt-hours of usable electricity. *Photo courtesy of Shell Solar.*

extra negative electrons, and the boron-doped silicon is called p-type for the extra positive holes. Now, if we take our silicon crystals, slice them into thin wafers, and carefully affix the n-type wafer to the p-type wafer, something interesting happens, and we're getting very close to having a useful electronic device.

Life at the P-N Junction

At first blush you might think that all the extra electrons in the n-type silicon would zoom across the p-n junction (the place where the two opposite types of silicon meet) and fill in all the holes in the p-type silicon, but it just doesn't happen that way. Oh, a lot of them start out fast enough, but quickly begin to have second thoughts. *Sure, an electron soon realizes, there may be a nice cozy place for me on the p-side, but my faithful proton is still on the n-side. I'm so confused.* It's a bit like young love.

The important thing to remember is that, even though n-type and p-type silicon have extra electrons and holes, neither type, alone, has any net electric charge. In both cases there are just enough electrons to balance out the protons. But once the two types of silicon are joined and the rush across the border occurs, that quickly changes. Every time an n-type electron jumps through the p-n junction and fills in a p-type hole, a negative charge is created on the p-side, while a positive charge springs up on the n-side in the place where the electron was, but no longer is. Once everything settles down, we find that there is a great gathering at the p-n junction, with negative electrons lining up along the p-side, and positive holes lining up along the n-side. This creates an electrical equilibrium, and if we left things like that the p-n junction would be a really boring place.

But we're not through yet, for now it's time to finish building our solar cell. To do this, we need to crisscross the surfaces of each of our

Pass Me That Really Good Silicon Glue, Please

Have you been wondering how they attach p-type silicon to n-type silicon? Glue, maybe? The fact is, it's all the same silicon wafer, oppositely doped on either side by a painstakingly-exacting process that gives the single piece of silicon the same properties as two perfectly-joined pieces.

silicon wafers with electrically-conducting channels. This will provides an easy path for the electrons to travel along, once we add the magical ingredient, sunlight.

When a photon of light of the right energy and wavelength strikes an electron hanging out with all of his buddies on the p-side of the p-n junction, the electron is instantly imbued with a jolt of energy and is suddenly free to move around. Where does it go? It can't go any farther into the p-side; there's quite a crowd there already. So instead it uses all this free energy to make a beeline back to the n-side. And, with a little luck, it will be picked up by one of the conductors on the surface of the n-layer and sent through an electrical circuit.

A Loopy Idea

Once the process begins, the electrical equilibrium at the p-n junction is hopelessly undone and the proverbial floodgates are opened. In an instant, multitudes of electrons that were just moments before hanging out at the p-n junction, are whisked out of their silicon Shangri-la, drawn through the windings of a washing machine motor or the filament of a light bulb,

BP solar modules and a PV Powered inverter are grid-connected on this home in Bend, Oregon. *Photo courtesy of Sunlight Solar Energy, Bend, OR.*

and unceremoniously dumped back on the p-side of the solar cell, totally exhausted. But, like battered and beaten heroes in a video game, all they really need is a little nourishment—a single photon—to be right back in the thick of things.

The completed circuit is the key to making the whole thing work. Since a solar cell acts as a diode—only letting the current flow from the p-side to the n-side—it wouldn't produce electricity for very long without a fresh supply of electrons continually re-entering the solar cell from the p-side. That's why all solar panels have positive and negative terminals. The electrons flow out of the negative terminal which conducts electrons from the n-type silicon, through the load (the above-mentioned washing machine or light bulb) and back into the p-type silicon via the positive terminal.

It's Practically Efficient

This, then, is how sunlight is harnessed to brew your coffee and run your big-screen High-Definition TV with quad-surround-sound. It's sunlight, in fact, that's providing the power to run the computer I'm using to write these words. It spares me the anguish of slowly going buggy while pecking away on a manual typewriter.

How efficient is the process? While efficiencies of over 25 percent have been achieved in the lab, most commercial panels operate at a peak efficiency of around 15 percent. This means that 15 of every 100 photons send electrons careening through the circuit. The other 85 are either absorbed as heat, or reflected back into the atmosphere.

Is that sufficiently efficient? Sure; from a practical standpoint, it's plenty. Many people—myself included—harvest all the power they need with a 100 to 200 square-foot solar array. That's less than the roof area of a small toolshed.

The only questions that remain are: what type of panels should you buy, and where should you put them?

But before we get to that point, we need to discuss the different types of grid-tied systems, and which one will work best for you. ❖

CHAPTER FOUR

You Want Batteries With That?

G rid-tie systems don't need batteries to function, but if you want instant emergency back-up power and the ability to keep using any available solar energy when the normal utility power fails, you'll be needing a battery bank. This is the major fork in system design, because much of the hardware required for battery-based systems is different from what's required for direct-intertie systems. Let's give a quick overview of your options.

Direct Grid-Tie Systems (without batteries)

Direct grid-tie (or intertie) is the simplest, least-expensive, and most efficient way to put a solar electric grid-tie system together. It's the path that about 95 percent of system owners have chosen to date. Direct-intertie systems treat the utility

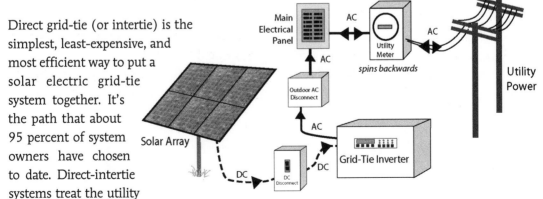

Solar Grid-Tie without Batteries

grid like a battery to absorb any extra, or make up any shortfall of energy. However...if utility power fails, your solar electric system shuts down—even if it's sunny daytime. Direct-intertie systems don't have any storage mechanism, other than the grid, and if it fails they will shut off almost instantly for safety. Direct-intertie probably won't work, or at least shouldn't be asked to work, with a back-up generator either. That's too small a "grid," and the generator probably won't react fast enough, or accurately enough, to keep the inverter from shutting off anyway.

Battery-Based Systems

Battery-based systems use a special inverter that can manage batteries and grid power simultaneously. So long as grid power is available they act pretty much just like a direct-intertie inverter, passing any extra

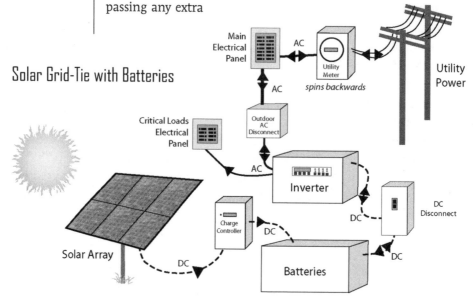

Solar Grid-Tie with Batteries

energy off to the grid, or letting the grid make up any shortfall. But if grid power fails, the inverter switches instantly to battery power (well, it actually takes about 20 milliseconds), and continues merrily on its way running anything connected to the inverter. These systems tend to be about 3 – 5 percent less efficient than direct-intertie systems at delivering the available PV wattage to your house. That's the price for keeping a set of batteries charged and ready to step in instantly to support selected circuits in your house. The size of your PV array, and/or how much household stuff you want to keep running, determines your inverter size. The size of your battery bank is determined by how long you want to run that household stuff when the grid fails. Battery banks can be very small, starting out at $200 to $300, or very large, exceeding $20,000, depending on your needs and budget.

You Can't Take It All With You

Battery-based systems usually don't try to back-up your entire household. We pick a few important circuits, like the fridge, furnace, office, a few lights and live with it. This keeps the battery bank more reasonably-sized, and lets the system run longer on what power is available. These systems could certainly be sized to run your whole house, and a system like that would sure make your installer's month a happy one. Americans don't tend to be energy conservative, so for most folks that would be a very expensive convenience. Back-up generators can easily be incorporated into battery-based systems for longer-term use. The generator can make up any energy shortfall by recharging the batteries periodically, and will probably only need to be run for a few hours every few days. There's no reason a system like this couldn't continue for months or even years without utility power.

The back-up abilities of these inverters is nearly instantaneous with most types of grid failure. They take over so fast that often you

The Right Tool for the Job

Batteries are built with different chemistries depending on what type of service they'll see. Automotive batteries enjoy a short, ugly life if put into off-grid deep-cycle service, for instance. If regular wet-cell deep-cycle batteries are put into emergency back-up service, a similar mismatch happens. It takes a special kind of battery to thrive under emergency back-up conditions. And that battery tends to be a sealed type.

won't even be aware that the grid has failed. This is good and bad. Good, because your computer won't crash. Bad, because if you don't know you're running on the back-up batteries, there's no reason to be conservative with power use. Switching time is usually under 1/100th of a second. For most home computers this is no sweat. The computer power supply can usually coast through at least 1/20th of a second. However! Be forewarned. No back-up inverter manufacturer claims that their units will act as an uninterruptible power supply

Why Your Back-up Inverter Is Not a UPS

A UPS, or uninterruptible power supply, is the $100 gizmo you plug your home or office computer into (if you or your boss is smart) that keeps your computer from instantly crashing when the power hiccups. If you opt for an intertie system with batteries, you'll have a system that seems to just be a great big UPS. After all, it takes over instantly if the grid goes down, right? Well, yes…most of the time. However, there are some kinds of grid failures that will cause your backup inverter to shut down. Let me tell you a tale of woe.

Back in the mid '90s when the first generation of Trace Engineering SW-series inverters came out, Real Goods set one up as a UPS for their phones and computer systems. If the utility failed, we'd have two to three hours of backup battery power, and the ability to plug in a generator to keep going. We figured we had a big powerful UPS for cheap.

Months later, across town, while installing major power for a large shopping center, the contractor had one of those "oops!" moments that very briefly resulted in many of the town's 120-volt circuits becoming 208 volts. Lights flared, but major breakers opened quickly, sparing most folks any damage. At Real Goods, our lights flared, and then everything went back to normal…uh, except that the phones and computers weren't working! For a "mail order" company in the 1990s, that's the equivalent of "dead."

The SW inverter, upon seeing over 170 volts input, had simply shut off to protect itself. Nice for the inverter, not at all nice for the Unix-based main-frame computer it was supposed to be protecting. Very bad things happen to Unix computers if they're crashed unexpectedly. Very bad things! It was hours before the Information Services crew got our ordering system up, and weeks later, plus hundreds of hours of overtime, before it was right again.

The moral of this story is, if you don't want to crash your computer, buy yourself a $100 UPS, even if you've already got a battery-based backup system.

– Doug Pratt

(UPS). There are some kinds of particularly nasty power failures that can cause the inverter to shut down to protect itself. I know. I've been there *(see story on the previous page).*

It Costs Extra and Doesn't Last Forever

Batteries are the one component of your system that will wear out and need replacement, typically at about ten-year intervals, but it depends on the quality of your battery bank. Batteries will last from five to twenty years, with the difference mostly in initial quality and size. Batteries are one of the few things in life where bigger really is better. Larger banks with 15- to 20-year life expectancies are available...for a price. Batteries are also going to need two to four hours of attention and maintenance on a yearly basis. On average you'll find that with the different inverter, extra controls, safety equipment, plus the cost of the batteries themselves, a battery-based system will probably cost about $3,000 to $5,000 more than the same PV array configured for direct grid-tie.

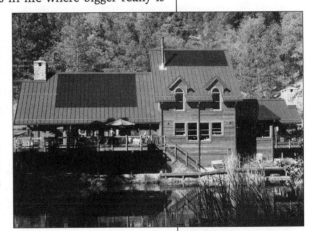

A PV system using Uni-Solar's peel-and-stick thin-film modules on metal roofing. The dark areas are the solar modules. *Photo courtesy of DC Power Systems.*

Which Is Right For Me?

Batteries or not...this depends mostly on how reliable the grid is in your area, and how much you'll suffer without it. If you can practically depend on regular, lengthy power outages (the hurricane-prone coastal regions of the southeastern U.S. come to mind), then back-up batteries are for you. If you only foresee one or two outages a year, and they're usually brief, then there's little incentive for the extra cost, maintenance, and eventual replacement of a battery bank. Buy a good UPS for your computer, and maybe a propane-fueled back-up generator if you're really concerned. Put your money into more PV wattage instead. It'll do you more good.

How A Backup Power System Saved My Bacon (and my Turkey)

It was 2:00 p.m. on Thanksgiving Day and all twelve members of my local family were at my house when the power went out. Did you know that modern pilotless gas ovens don't work without electricity? It's a fact that about two-thirds of our small town of 15,000 souls was about to learn, because the power stayed off for most folks until about 9:00 p.m. that evening. Suffice it to say, there were many ruined dinners and short tempers that day.

At my house? Thanks to some excess paranoia concerning Y2K, I had equipped myself with an inverter that would plug into the battery bank of my electric vehicle. I had 10 kWh of stored energy sitting in the driveway, and the means to deliver it to my house! No problem! Within five minutes I had the inverter plugged in and the house switched over to backup mode. The silent inverter happily ran the oven, the fridge, the furnace, the microwave, some lights, even the TV for traditional football. We had the only lights on in the neighborhood, and no generator noise. We weren't the least bit inconvenienced and a memorable dinner arrived on time.

– Doug Pratt

Seal Them Up!

We strongly recommend sealed batteries for emergency back-up battery banks. Why? A couple reasons. 1) We've found from hard experience that batteries tend to be forgotten and neglected, and emergency battery banks especially so. Wet cell batteries need watering every three to four months and, despite all the best intentions, they will be forgotten. This leads to sharply-reduced life expectancy and performance. 2) Wet cell batteries are like the muscles of your body. They need exercise in order to stay healthy. If batteries aren't cycled regularly they become stiff and resistant chemically. They won't be able to deliver the power when they're finally asked to. Imagine what kind of shape you'd be in if you spent two years strapped to a bed and then got thrown out the door to run a marathon. Yeah, ugly isn't it? Sealed batteries never need watering, and their chemistry and construction is tweaked a bit because they expect to spend long periods doing nothing, and then suddenly get asked to work their heart out. They still won't be real happy about it, but they'll tolerate it fairly well. Sealed batteries are more expensive than conventional wet cells, but for emergency back-up, this is money well spent! (*Read more in chapters 5 and 11.*) ❖

Sun-Xtender® sealed battery by Concorde. *Photo courtesy of Concorde Batteries.*

A 5.76 kW array was installed on this horse barn in Woodstock, Vermont in 1999. Note the steep PV mounting angle for northern latitudes. The grid-tied system has 48 BP solar panels, dual Xantrex SW5548 inverters and 24 Surrette batteries for 35 kWh of storage. *Photo courtesy of Global Resource Options, White River Junction, Vermont.*

Doug's Disappearing Solar

The 48 Uni-Solar peel-and-stick panels on Doug Pratt's garage are nearly invisible, but the 20 kWh per day of electricity (on average) that it provides is quite noticeable, as is evidenced by the zero electric bills from his utility company. In Doug's own words:

"We decided to install a battery-based system because lengthy power outages aren't uncommon in our rural area, and with the nice California rebate we could afford to spend a bit more for the security. In my power room foreground you see the sealed batteries with a wooden cover so nothing can get dropped on them. On the

wall, there's pair of Outback 3,600-watt inverters with a DC box and a pair of the superb MX60 charge controls on the near side, and an AC box on the far side for all the wiring and safety gear. Further down the wall there's a pair of standard circuit breaker boxes. One is for utility power, the other for inverter power. Note they're connected by a gutter box so individual circuits could be easily moved if we change our mind about what wants backup power.

"In our present home we use about 8 to 10 kWh per day. When we build our new energy-efficient, passive-solar home, we'll use a ground-coupled heat pump for heating and cooling. Even at regular electric rates these pumps are the least expensive way to heat and cool a house, but with all of my extra free electric power, it'll be no problem to run a pump! Electricity, heat, and cooling with no impact on my children...I can live with that!"

Photos by Doug Pratt.

CHAPTER FIVE

Sizing Your System

B efore I began writing a monthly column about people who live with solar and wind energy, I figured everyone should install the biggest renewable energy (RE) system they could afford, right up to the point where all of their electrical energy needs were covered most of the time, without resorting to a backup generator or the power grid. Though I still think it's a good idea, I've come to the realization that most people think differently than I do about this matter. I've met people with huge RE systems who, because they refuse to adopt a more energy-efficient lifestyle, still rely heavily on grid power, or, if living off-grid, generator power. Others are happy with one or two panels and a couple of batteries to run a small TV or computer, and simply do without electricity for everything else. To each their own.

Still, most of us install our systems for a particular purpose—to provide backup power during grid outages, for instance—and sizing such systems requires a fair bit of planning based on reliable data.

Hidden Savings

If you generate one kWh of your own electricity, you save much more than one kWh from the utility company. Over 3.3 kWh of energy were consumed to deliver that one kWh to your home.

Different Strokes for Different Folks (with different systems)

Direct grid-tie systems without batteries do not provide any power when the grid goes down, so they can be as big or as small as you

Carbon Dioxide Carriers
Replace five 60-watt incandescent light bulbs (each burning 5 hours per day) with 12-watt compact fluorescent bulbs, and you'll offset the burning of nearly 440 pounds of coal and over 860 pounds of CO_2 going into the atmosphere **each year**. If a million people did this for 20 years, the CO_2 not sent up the smokestack would outweigh 77 Nimitz Class aircraft carriers, each boasting a displacement of 102,000 metric tons!

desire, or as your pocketbook permits. Why are you installing this type of system? If it's because you want to pitch in and do your part to offset the burning of tons of coal, or to reduce the size of the growing mountain of radioactive wastes produced by nuclear fission, then your decision is a simple monetary one: buy whatever you can afford. On the other hand, if you hope to see a credit on your bill from the power company now and then, you'll need to do some figuring.

Are you planning a system with batteries? If so, the planning stage becomes more critical, since you will need to know, at a bare minimum: 1) How much power is consumed by the appliances and home systems you wish to keep operating when the grid goes down; 2) How many watts of solar capacity it will take in your particular geographical area to keep the batteries at an acceptable state of charge during a power outage; 3) How big of an inverter you will need to provide power to the loads it will be running; and 4) How big of a battery bank will be required to power your home during a power outage.

You'll also need to know where you're going to put all the components, since batteries take up a fair bit of room and need to be as close to the inverter as possible.

But I'm getting ahead of myself.

Watt(s) You Use versus Watt(s) You Need

A quick glance at your monthly bill from Planet Power Conglomerated will tell you how many kilowatt hours of electricity you used in any given billing cycle, and a little math will give your daily usage. That's the easy part, and if you're willing to spend $4 to $5 per watt on the solar panels required to maintain your current degree of consumption, then simply plug that figure into the system-sizing table in the appendix and don't give it another thought.

But before you get the shock to your wallet that option delivers, you might want to examine how you use your electricity, since your house is probably full of energy-sucking devices and appliances. This is because electricity has traditionally been so cheap that manufacturers have had little incentive to incur the added expense of engineering and producing energy-efficient products.

The biggies are obvious: refrigerators and freezers, air conditioning, forced-air heat, electric ranges, water heaters and clothes dryers. But there are also many little things we don't usually consider that, taken as a whole, can make a big difference. Light bulbs, for instance. Every 60-watt incandescent bulb you replace with an equivalent compact fluorescent bulb using only 12 watts will save you 0.048 kWh for each hour it's turned on. If you switch out 5 light bulbs that burn an average of 5 hours per day, you can knock 36 kWh per month (1.20 kWh/day) off your electrical consumption. This is enough energy savings to run a reasonably-efficient (note that I did not say "expensive super-efficient"), off-the-shelf refrigerator 24/7 and still have a few kilowatts hours to spare at the end of each month.

How many electrical devices and appliances do you have around the house that come with heavy, black, plug adapters? Those adapters or power cubes are actually rectifiers used to convert high-voltage AC to low-voltage DC. You will find them on laptop computers and many peripherals, cell-phone chargers and other chargers for portable devices, TV cable boxes, lamps, etc. They are also used internally in stereos, computers, battery chargers for portable tools, and so on. They all have one property in common: they draw power continuously—usually in the one- to four-watt range—for as long as they are plugged in, even if the power to the appliance is turned off. In fact, power companies don't call them power cubes; they officially call them "power vampires." How can you tell if your pet vampire is using electricity? If you don't have a usage meter to plug it in to—which is really the best way—simply touch it. If it's warm, it's using electricity. How do you

Energy Pigs

Not-so-old fridges are energy pigs. A typical new fridge now uses 80% less energy than a model from the late 1980s and early 90s.

Demand Keeps Growing

World energy consumption is projected to increase by 59% from 1999 to 2020. Much of that growth is expected in developing countries.

Source: SolarBuzz.com

stop these things from using electricity? Just plug them into a power strip and turn off that power! The savings over the long haul can be substantial.

Electric clocks are also accomplished watt thieves, usually drawing one to three watts continuously. I know it doesn't sound like much, but over the course of a year a 3-watt clock will consume in excess of 26 kWh of electricity. That's over a day's electrical consumption for an average house, just to power a timepiece that could be traded out for a battery-operated model that will run for two years on a single AA battery! I've often wondered what the designers of battery-operated clocks know that the plug-in guys don't.

Okay—so much for the little stuff. Now you have to ask yourself how many of the biggies you're willing to part with to make your excursion into solar energy a worthwhile venture. Below are the average power-consumption values for some downright piggish electrical appliances (*see the appendix for a more complete list*):

Electric clothes dryer	4,000 watts
Electric range	1,200–2,600 watts (per burner)
Electric water heater	4,500–5,500 watts
Central air conditioning	2,000–5,000 watts

Does it take an hour to dry your clothes? Kiss goodbye to 4 kWh of electricity. This is roughly equal to the average daily output of a 1,200-watt solar array in a sunny climate at mid latitudes. Fortunately, a natural-gas or propane-powered dryer uses 1/10th that amount of electricity, and burning natural gas or propane in your home is far more environmentally benign than burning coal to make electricity at some distant power plant. The stove and water heater can likewise be replaced with gas models. Is your fridge more than five years old?

New models are so much more efficient they'll pay for themselves in a few years. (To see just how efficient the new models are, check out *www.energystar.gov*.)

This leaves us with the biggest pig on the whole farm, central air conditioning. How badly do you need it, really? Could you go through a summer with a swamp cooler, or a few fans, instead? Before you answer, you might want to complete the system-sizing worksheet in the appendix, with and without the central air. The difference could give you the chills.

Building a new home? Look into ground-coupled or geothermal heat pumps. They are by far the least expensive cooling and heating sources now available. Of course, by designing your home to take advantage of passive solar heating and lighting, then building it tight and insulating it well, you'll set yourself up for a lifetime of energy savings.

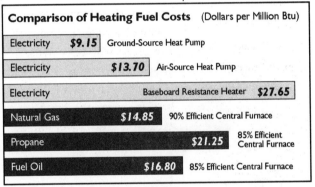

Comparison of Heating Fuel Costs   (Dollars per Million Btu)

Electricity	**$9.15**	Ground-Source Heat Pump
Electricity	**$13.70**	Air-Source Heat Pump
Electricity	Baseboard Resistance Heater	**$27.65**
Natural Gas	**$14.85**	90% Efficient Central Furnace
Propane	**$21.25**	85% Efficient Central Furnace
Fuel Oil	**$16.80**	85% Efficient Central Furnace

Fuel Costs are late 2004 averages: Electricity $0.0934 / kWh; Natural Gas $13.78 / thousand cubic feet; Fuel Oil $2.00 / gallon; Propane $1.65 / gallon

Sizing the Components: Inverters and Charge Controllers

Now that you know where most of your energy is going and what you can do to slow the flood of watts to a manageable stream, it's time to think about system size. For direct grid-tied systems without charge controllers and batteries, your only real concern is making certain that your inverter is big enough to handle the wattage generated by your solar array. Are you thinking of adding more solar panels down the road? You could get a bigger inverter now, or you could buy an inverter well-suited to your initial array, and add a second inverter when you get around to increasing your solar capacity.

For systems with batteries, your initial planning is more critical. Once you determine the size of your solar array *(see the worksheets in the appendix)*, you can match it up with a proportionately-sized battery bank and charge controller. The inverter, on the other hand, is sized to meet the demands on the AC side of things, so unless you add onto your house or increase the loads you'll be running, the inverter you begin with will more than likely serve you well, even if the rest of your system suffers from occasional growing pains.

Charge controllers—at least the ordinary garden variety—are fairly inexpensive and if you need to add another one when you enlarge your array, you won't be out too much money. But if your initial array is capable of, say, 35 amps, and you suspect you may want to add onto it someday, your money might be better spent in buying a 60-amp charge controller, rather than a 40-amp model.

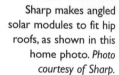

Sharp makes angled solar modules to fit hip roofs, as shown in this home photo. *Photo courtesy of Sharp.*

How Many Batteries?

A battery bank is a bit tougher to size. Ideally, you will want to have enough battery power to get you through a world-class power outage in the midst of a cloudy spell, without running your batteries below

50 percent capacity. But this isn't always realistic. Batteries take up a lot more space than other indoor components. For instance, MK's 8G31 12-volt sealed gel-type batteries—a tried-and-true favorite among grid-tied renewable energy enthusiasts—take up roughly one square foot of floor space for every 2 kWh of *usable* capacity. So, if the systems you're running require 10 kWh per day and you want enough battery capacity for 3 days, you'll need to find at least 15 square feet of unused space to put your batteries.

And if you should want to add more batteries later? Your batteries will need to be purchased in sets of two or four and the size of the sets will be based on your system voltage. Why? Battery-based systems usually operate at 12, 24, or 48 volts, the latter two being by far the most common. If your batteries are of the 12-volt persuasion (as with the above-mentioned MK batteries), you will need to wire them in series to achieve the system voltage you want: a 24-volt system requires that batteries be installed in sets of two, while a 48-volt system takes batteries in sets of four. If you instead opt for 6-volt batteries, these numbers will be doubled. The only way around this mathematical conundrum is to buy an MPPT charge controller that allows you to run a 24-volt system from a 48- or 60-volt array (*see the section on MPPT charge controllers, page 118-119*).

Doug's sealed 48-volt / 555-amp hour battery bank can deliver a very comfortable 13.5 kWh at 50% depth of discharge, and requires 5 minutes of maintenance per year. It's shipped in 6-packs with solid soldered interconnects between cells (visible in the center), which you see here with nice, safe plastic covers over them. Non-removable caps provide a one-way vent if the batteries are over-charged. Life expectancy is about 15 years. *Photo by Doug Pratt.*

System Voltage

In the early days of solar, most systems were on backwoods shanties and were comprised of a couple of panels and two or four batteries. These systems usually operated at 12 volts because that's the voltage needed by the RV lights most people were using back then. But things have changed. Today's components are far more sophisticated and, watt for watt, are considerably cheaper. We want to run more than just a few lights and a small TV; we'd like to rival the wattage we buy from the power company.

For reasons discussed earlier *(see chapter 3)*, higher voltage translates to higher efficiencies. The wires running from a 48-volt array need only be 1/4th the size of the wires needed for a 24-volt array, and 1/16th the size required by a 12-volt array. Likewise, a 48-volt inverter will operate more efficiently than a 24- or 12-volt inverter. And these days most large solar panels are wired for 24-volt operation, which means it only takes two panels wired in series to make a 48-volt array.

The higher the voltage the better, then. Many direct grid-tied systems operate at several hundred volts, depending on which inverter you choose. For battery-based systems 24- and 48-volts is the norm, with 48-volts beginning to take the lead in newer systems.

Are you planning a battery-based system? Do you have the room (and the funds) to increase the size of your battery bank four (or eight, for 6-volt batteries) batteries at a time? Then go with 48 volts. You can't go wrong. ❖

A 1.5 kW array feeds a sub-panel on this home office in South Strafford, Vermont. The electricity is then routed to the main house for their non-battery, grid-tied system. *Photo courtesy of Global Resource Options, White River Junction, Vermont.*

CHAPTER SIX

Where Does Everything Go?

W here can you—and can't you—put your solar array, batteries, inverter(s) and charge controller(s)? I'd like to say simply that everything except the solar array has to go inside, but that's not exactly true, so here it is, caveats and all.

Where Should I Put My Solar Array?

Since your solar array will be located outside, space is usually not a problem unless you've got a huge array and a tiny house. Crystalline silicon panels will take up about one square foot of space for every 10 – 12 watts of power they produce; amorphous silicon panels over half-again that much area. So, if you've calculated you'll need a 3,000-watt array, you can mount it on 300 square feet of roof if you are using crystalline panels, or 450 – 550 square feet of roof for amorphous panels, shingles, or standing-seam solar roof panels. Since most residential roofs are over 1,500 square feet, finding a place for you array should not be a problem if a good portion of your roof faces south. Likewise with ground- or deck-mounted arrays.

There seems to be an almost universal misconception among those who have never had PV equipment that the array has to go on the roof. It doesn't. In fact, in many instances you're better off

Face the Sun

In the northern hemisphere, your PV array wants to face due south, but there's some wiggle room. Within 25 degrees of true south, you'll still collect 98% of the sun's energy.

mounting it on terra firma. It's easier to wash the panels when they're at ground level, easier to sweep away snow in winter, and easier to make seasonal adjustments to the tilt angle.

Mounting the array on the outside of a south-facing deck is another option, albeit not a very aesthetically pleasing one. The payoff is in the fact that it's even easier to clean a deck-mounted array than one at ground level. And it will be less likely that the kid you pay to keep the weeds at bay with a weed wacker will send a rock careening at Mach 2 into one of your expensive panels.

A solar array mounted on a south-facing deck (left) and another array mounted on the ground makes for easy snow removal (right). *Photos by LaVonne Ewing.*

But we don't all have big, sunny yards or decks, and for you it may be the roof or nothing. If your roof is composed of composition shingles or standing-seam metal panels, it should be a fairly straight-forward job. It is not difficult to seal-up around the places where the bolts penetrate through a composition shingle roof, and for standing-seam metal roofs there are now non-penetrating mounts available.

Wood shingles are a bit more challenging, owing to the fact that they have a tendency to split. For these types of roofs we strongly recommend stand-off type supports with an impermeable flashing that's designed for wood shingles. You might want to consult a good roofer to make sure it's done right.

Tile, either clay or concrete, is another step up the ladder of difficulty. As an erstwhile roofer, I can attest to the recalcitrant nature

Pole-mounted arrays are easy to adjust to the optimum sun angle. *Photo by LaVonne Ewing.*

Avoid the Shade

Shading is far more important than direction. If turning east or west helps you avoid shading, go for it!

Tilt to Meet the Sun

The sun passes through 47 degrees of latitude in its journey from the Tropic of Capricorn on the first day of winter (December 21), to the Tropic of Cancer on the first day of Summer (June 21). This means that the angle at which sunlight hits your array is constantly changing. And, unless, you adjust your array to keep it perpendicular—or nearly so—to the incoming light, the array's efficiency will wax and wane right along with the seasons.

If you have a ground-mounted array supported from a central pole, you will be able to adjust the angle fairly easily; just place an angle finder on the array, remove a couple of bolts, tilt the array to the desired angle, and replace the bolts into different holes. But how do you know what angle is optimal?

On March 20 and September 22 (the vernal and autumnal equinoxes) when night and day are the same length everywhere in the world, your array angle should be equal to your latitude. Then as the seasons change, you can increase or decrease the angle to ensure your array is always delivering as much wattage as possible.

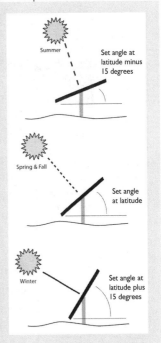

of tile roofs. That being said, they're not impossible; they simply require an extra measure of thought and caution. There are mounting systems made especially for tile roofs *(see chapter 11)*, and in many areas these mounting systems are required.

If you'd rather go about it the old-fashioned way (and local codes permit), you can have a roofer remove the tile where the supports meet the roof and install a rubberized flashing (or some other membrane-type roofing material). The flashing is attached to the roof deck underneath the tiles above the array support, and then glued to the top of the lower tiles. A fair bit of work, yes, but not terribly difficult for a roofer who's been around awhile. Find one sprouting a few gray hairs—it's a cinch he's not new to the trade.

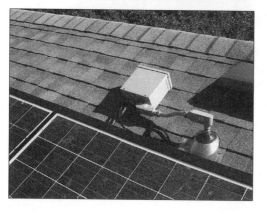

Your PV array is going to last 50 to 80 years, so lay a good foundation! **Top Left:** A securely-installed standoff, bolted to a roof framing member. **Above:** All-metal flashings that are caulked around the top. Also shown: a splice bar on the top rail, and a ground wire (on the lower standoff) waiting for PV modules. **Left:** Newer style of flashing with a no-caulk rubber insert. The junction box will provide space to convert the MC connector cables to conventional (less expensive) wiring before dropping down to the inverter area. *Photos courtesy of Affinity Energy, Windsor, CA.*

Making Space for the Batteries, Inverters and Other Stuff

How much space does it all take? As I mentioned above, MK batteries require roughly one square foot for every two usable kWh of stored energy. Less powerful batteries may take up twice that much space. Bigger, more efficient batteries are available, but they require a commensurately greater investment. Many people find room for batteries under work benches, others build very sturdy shelves to stack them. There are only three requirements for locating your batteries: 1) They need to be as close to the inverter as possible; 2) The batteries cannot, however, be located directly under the inverter; 3) Wet lead-acid batteries must be in a sealed room or box—as opposed to sealed batteries, which need not be sequestered—and must be vented to the outside, since they give off highly-flammable hydrogen gas when they get worked up.

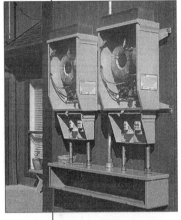

A pair of PV Powered grid-tie inverters (with their covers removed for wiring) mounted on an exterior wall. *Photo courtesy of PV Powered.*

Compared to the batteries and the solar array, the rest is small change, topographically speaking. Even if you're planning a pair of inverters and charge controllers, you should be able to fit it all on a half-sheet (4-foot x 4-foot) of ¾-inch plywood mounted to the wall—which is far preferable to direct wall mounting of the components, owing to the fact that inverters for battery-based systems are exceedingly weighty beasts (upwards of 100 pounds). Besides, wall studs are like cops: you can never find one when you need one.

There is a big difference between direct grid-tie inverters and battery-based inverters when it comes to finding a place to put them. Direct grid-tie inverters are happiest if they're mounted outside, but you've got to find a shady spot for them, since they will limit their output to control their internal temperature, should they get too hot. Unshaded south- and west-facing walls, then, are a bad idea, while north-facing walls are perfect—as long as you don't cover them up just because they're not pretty to look at. They've got to

Running Your Solar
Circuits Circuitiously

Your wire runs might
be longer than you
anticipated if your meter
is located on a distant
pole and the local utility
requires a solar DC
disconnect within
10 feet of it. Rather than
doing a marathon wire
run from the array, to
the meter, to the
inverter, many choose
instead to install a
whole-house disconnect
at the meter. (See
chapter 11 for details.)

have air. Can't find a suitable outside location for your direct grid-tie inverter? Buy a model with an internal fan; these units can safely be mounted in a garage or utility room.

Battery-based inverters are a different matter. They *must* be mounted in a building out of the elements. Does this building need to be climate controlled? No, it doesn't; inverters can handle reasonable extremes in temperature. But you don't want to put one in a barn with dust and snow blowing through the cracks in the walls, either.

Many people find it convenient to locate their components in tightly-built sheds beyond the house, then run the AC to the house via a buried cable. It gets everything out of the way, and ensures that they don't have to listen to the hum of the inverter, which can get a bit distracting when it's really working.

The only problem we have with this arrangement is the fact that the batteries have to be in the same general location as the inverter, and battery performance drops with the mercury. How much?

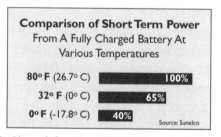

Comparison of Short Term Power
From A Fully Charged Battery At
Various Temperatures

80° F (26.7° C)	100%
32° F (0° C)	65%
0° F (-17.8° C)	40%

Source: Sunelco

Between 80° Fahrenheit (26.7° C) and freezing (32° Fahrenheit, or 0° C) short-term power availability drops off by a third. Go down to 0° Fahrenheit (-17.8° C) and your battery efficiency drops to 40 percent. It's something to keep in mind.

Ideally, then, you'll want to mount your components inside your house, unless you're contemplating a direct grid-tied system, in which case outside is best. But where inside? Non-living areas in basements are ideal, as are workshops and garages. Basically any dry, secluded area where the hum of the inverter will not be a distraction. On the other hand, if you locate the inverter in the closet of the guest bedroom, you can practically be guaranteed that your in-laws' visits will be short ones.

How Far Away Can It Be?

If you decide to locate all of your components in a shed a good ways distant from the house or, conversely, to place your solar array very far to the south of the house (and the inverter), your only real constraint is voltage loss though the wires. The farther electricity has to travel through a wire, the greater the losses due to resistance within the wire (remember?). How much loss can you afford? You absolutely, positively, do not want your voltage to drop by more than 2 percent from point A to point B. The reason is that a drop in voltage is accompanied by a corresponding drop in amperage, which will be even greater than the loss in voltage. You're investing a lot of money in your system—there's no point in sacrificing your hard-earned watts to skinny wire.

So, again, voltage is good. A 48-volt array, for instance, will safely deliver 1,200 watts a distance of 184 feet through 1/0 wire; a 24-volt array can only push that much current 46 feet with minimal loss. Of course, if you are planning a direct grid-tied system operating at several hundred volts, then you have a great deal more latitude in where you place your array.

The same is true for distant inverters. What's true for DC holds for AC, so if you run 120-volt AC to the house from an inverter in a shed, you will get better than a four-fold boost in the wire's carrying capacity over the 48 volts from your array. But before you get too heady, remember that you will sending much more wattage from the inverter to the house than from the array to the inverter, since you will have to size your wire to match the surge output of the inverter, a considerable amount of current for a reasonably-sized inverter.

The bottom line? Plan ahead. Before you decide

Fancy stuff! This house has large, multiple PV arrays that don't all face the same direction; hence, multiple inverters. A 3,500-watt Sharp SunVista inverter sits below a Sunny Boy 2500. DC disconnects are on the upper left, and a small AC breaker panel on the lower left combines both inverters' outputs so a single AC disconnect switch can be used at the utility meter (not shown) to keep those busy utility folks happy. Don't like all the shiny conduit? Paint it before installation, or use plastic. *Photo courtesy of Affinity Energy, Windsor, CA.*

to locate your array or inverter on that sunny spot south of the distant knoll, stop to calculate how much you'll be paying for the wire that's going to be delivering the current. ❖

Doing What It Takes To Be Self-Sufficient

Yes, living in New York does have its advantages. After Chris and Kimberly Andersen installed a direct grid-tie solar-electric system on their 2,200-square-foot home in Saratoga County, the State promptly sent the installer, Global Resource Options, a check for $15,000, the credit for which was reflected on the Andersen's bill. Then the State gave the homeowners an income tax credit and also bought down their loan to a comfortable 1.5 percent interest. At the rate they're cutting their monthly electric bills, the system will have largely paid for itself by the time the loan matures in 10 years.

What did the Andersens and NYSERDA (New York State Energy Research and Development Authority) invest in? An array of two dozen 160-watt BP solar panels on a UniRac roof mount and a pair of Sunny Boy 1800U inverters. During the first year the system has been in operation, the Andersens were able to slice 75 percent off their electric bill, but they are hoping for more. By installing double-glazed low E argon-filled windows, compact fluorescent light bulbs and high-efficiency appliances—the latter also partly subsidized by the State—Chris and Kim hope to conserve enough in the coming years to cut their electric bill to zero.

Why did they do it? Chris says, simply, "We wanted to do what we could be become self-sufficient." Chris spent time in Botswana with the Peace Corps before meeting Kim. The couple—both educators in the public school system—then lived in Paraguay for awhile after tying the knot. These are two places where limitless electricity and modern conveniences are in short supply.

Do they have any desire to emulate the lifestyle of a developing country? Of course not; they just see no reason why they and their two small children should have to consume any more natural resources than necessary.

Photo by the Andersens

CHAPTER SEVEN
Got Wind?

D o you live out of town on a nice little acreage where you spend more time listening to the wind soughing through the trees than you do listening to your neighbors banging around across the fence? You should consider yourself fortunate; if that ol' north wind is strong enough, it could go a long way toward lowering your electric bills and powering your home during blackouts.

Wind power is not for everyone, of course. In many areas of the U.S. the force of the wind near ground level is too slight to be of practical value for a home-based wind system. And even if you do have usable wind power where you live, other factors need to be considered before you rush out and buy a wind system.

Yea! The wind is blowing!

Have you spent your life cursing the wind? Installing a wind system is guaranteed to change your attitude.

A Matter of Geography

In addition to the wind itself, you will need to have enough land to safely locate the tower on which the turbine will be placed. Usually, this means an acre or more. Some folks are able to avoid installing a tower by mounting one or more small wind

Persuasive Math

Ever see a news story about a guy who refuses to leave his home, even after being told his house is about to be disassembled by a hurricane? I've often wondered what these hard cases would do if someone informed them that a 150-mph wind is not merely 3 times stronger than a 50-mph wind, as they probably imagine, but rather a rafter-rending 27 times stronger.

turbines (500 watts or less) on a barn or other non-living out-building, where the vibration caused by the spinning blades will not shake the plaster off the walls and induce periodic fits of insanity. However, for larger machines (600 watts and up), a tower is a must.

There are two things to keep in mind when searching out a spot to place a tower. First, it should be far enough away from living areas and property lines that no one would be injured (or worse) if the tower fell over, or if all or part of the wind turbine came flying off in a killer wind or microburst—worst-case scenario stuff, in other words. How far is far enough? A good rule of thumb is 15 rotor diameters away from the house, so if your turbine has, say, an 11-foot propeller, you'll want to place your tower at least 165 feet away.

Secondly, the tower should be high enough to clear any obstacles that might be in the path of the wind. Ideally, the turbine should be mounted at least 30 feet above the tallest object—tree, building, hill, etc.—within 300 feet. This requirement is to minimize the effects of air turbulence, which is to a wind turbine what a washboard road is to a car. Besides causing extra wear and tear on the turbine, turbulence greatly diminishes the force of the wind.

How Much Wind Is Enough?

So you've got land with an ideal location for a wind turbine, and neither your neighbors nor the local bureaucrats have any objections to a tower. Now you need to determine if you have enough wind at your site to justify the time and expense of installing a wind system. The first thing you will discover is that exact wind data for your particular location is probably non-existent, unless your home is next to an airport or a military base. But you can still get a pretty good idea what the force of the wind is in your area by referring to the wind maps for your state. The Department of Energy (DOE) maps at the Bergey

Windpower website (*www.bergey.com*) assign a wind class number to every square inch of every state. Though these maps are painted with a rather broad brush, they still offer a lot of insight for the wind resources that are available in your area. For further clarification, you should also read the National Renewable Energy Laboratory's Wind Energy Resource Atlas of the United States at *http://rredc.nrel.gov/ wind/pubs/atlas/chp1.html*. This is a thorough document that discusses national and regional wind patterns, seasonal variations, and the painstaking methods used to compile the data.

A quick glance at the national map *(see page 134)* will show you that the most paltry wind resources are in the Southeast, while large areas of excellent wind are in the upper Midwest, particularly the Dakotas and the western edge of Minnesota. Good winds can also be found in the higher terrain of both the Northeast and Northwest, and all along the Rocky Mountains.

You might also want to view the maps at the Southwest Windpower site (*www.windenergy.com*). Southwest has collected links to the best maps available for each state. Some were compiled by NREL, others by TrueWind Solutions. In some states you will be able to input geographical coordinates and print out an extensive data sheet showing, among other things, the average strength of the wind from 16 different directions, as well as the average wind speed and power density during different seasons and from varying heights above the earth's surface. Bear in mind, however, that this information results from extrapolation of existing data from the nearest sites where measurements actually were taken. No one really knows for sure what the wind characteristics are at the top of the tower you haven't erected yet.

To be absolutely sure there's enough wind at your site, you may want to buy an anemometer and monitor its readings for a few months. If you get a fancy recording anemometer, or one with a

Small Wind Turbines

In 2004, more than 7,400 wind turbines were manufactured in the U.S. and more than 40% were exported to overseas markets.

Southwest Windpower Whisper 100 (the re-engineered H40 model). *Photo courtesy of Southwest Windpower.*

Tax Credits and Rebates for Wind?

Yes, there are financial incentives for prospective wind farmers. In many cases, a home-based wind system is eligible for the same tax credits and rebates as a solar system. Check the sources discussed in chapter 9, as well as your state energy office listed in the appendix.

computer interface you will actually be able to plot wind patterns over time to determine what the average wind speed is at your location for different months of the year. Should you go this route, however, please bear in mind that your anemometer readings will not be entirely accurate unless you are able to mount the instrument at the same height as your proposed wind turbine. The lower you place it, the less encouraging your results.

Should you go this route, the folks at Iowa State University have compiled a Wind Energy Manual that will tell you, among other things, where best to locate your anemometer and how to extrapolate the data you collect to calculate probable wind speed at different heights above different types of terrain. You can download this handy document at: *www.energy.iastate.edu/renewable/wind/wem/wem-08_power.html.*

But you really shouldn't have to sort through mountains of data, or spend a lot of money on wind monitoring equipment, for the simple fact is, if you think you have enough wind at your site, in all likelihood you do. My own personal rule of thumb goes as follows:

> *If the wind at your site blows often enough and hard enough to annoy you, you probably have enough wind to make good use of a wind system.*

However you go about it, there are some surprising facts about wind speed and the amount of power you can hope to harvest from the wind. For starters, the relationship between the speed of the wind and the power it generates is not a simple linear correlation. What am I talking about? Just this: a 30 mph wind is not, as you might imagine, half-again as powerful as a 20 mph wind—it's nearly 3.4 times stronger! How can this be? It's because the force of the wind increases as the cube of the wind speed. So, 20 x 20 x 20 = 8,000, while 30 x 30 x 30 = 27,000. If you then multiply either of these products by 0.05472, you will discover the force of the wind in watts per square meter (W/m^2) at sea level for that particular wind speed. This is a tidy arrangement, because it turns out that solar radiation is also measured in W/m^2, so it's a simple matter to compare the speed of the wind hitting the blades of a turbine, with the sunlight that falls on an array.

And how do they compare with one another? Generally, the power of the sunlight hitting the earth (or your solar array) in the middle part of a summer's day at mid-latitudes is equal to a steady wind speed of 22 to 23 mph—about 600 W/m^2.

This isn't the amount of power you'll be sending to your house, how-ever. Your solar array will only be able to reap around 12 to 15 percent of this energy, and these figures hold fairly well for wind generators, too, though efficiency percentage is not a com-monly-used term with home-based wind turbines, owing to the fact that similarly-rated machines may have vastly different sweep areas.

A home in Norman, Oklahoma installed a Bergey 10kW Excel-S wind turbine as a grid-intertie system in 1983. The guyed-lattice tower is 100 feet tall. *Photo courtesy of Bergey Windpower.*

However you measure it, it takes a pretty stiff breeze—square meter for square meter—to rival the power of the sun; far more wind than is blowing around in most locations. Considering the psycho-logical effect wind has on a lot of people, this is probably a good thing. But it also makes your decision to install a wind system more difficult since you might live in a fringe area, where there may or may not be enough wind to make the installation of a tower and turbine a successful venture.

If the average annual wind speed where you live is 10 mph or more, you can almost be assured of having enough wind to reap a useful bounty of power from the unsettled atmosphere. This is because,

Doug's Detours

Big, heavy and slow aren't qualities we often look for in modern society, but they're great qualities in a wind turbine.

unlike a solar array, a wind generator's capacity to produce power is not limited to the hours between sunrise and sunset—it can produce power day or night, rain or shine.

The DOE maps list wind speed in power classes from 1 to 7. The upper limit of Class 1 winds approach 10 mph, provided the turbine is mounted high enough above ground. If you live in a Class 1 area you should probably do some homework before opting for a wind system. Living in a Class 2 area, though more promising than Class 1, does not assure you of enough wind, especially if your site is in a valley, near the lee side of a hill, or surrounded by towering trees (unless you are able to raise your tower at least 30 feet above the tallest nearby trees). By contrast, hilltops, coast lines and high plains make excellent sites for gathering wind.

We cannot over-emphasize the importance of tower height in designing a wind system. There really is a lot more wind up there, and it will invariably be steadier and less turbulent than the gusty, chaotic breezes that occur closer to terra firma. In fact, the DOE generally considers the wind power density at 50 meters (164 feet) to be double what it is at 10 meters (33 feet). The actual figures will vary over different types of terrain, of course, but it's still an eye-opening exercise in mathematics. You probably won't erect a 164-foot tower, but the DOE figures do make a point: height is good (just like voltage).

Whisper-ing in a Blizzard

In March 2003, Colorado was blasted by a drought-busting three-day blizzard. The snow piled up more than 3 feet on the level, with drifts of over 6 feet, completely covering cars and pickups, and solar arrays. Grid power went down in many places, and those around us who had solar with battery-backup eventually had to resort to their gas generators to keep things in the comfort zone. We, on the other hand, were basking in a power surplus, thanks to the steady 30-mph wind driving our trusty old Whisper 1000. Though we used electricity with giddy abandon (what else do you do when you can't go outside?) our battery level never dropped below 90 percent.

— Rex Ewing

Although most modern wind turbines begin to spin—and thereby produce some amount of power—at 6 to 7 mph (the "cut-in" wind speed), they will not really begin to produce much in the way of usable power below 8 or 9 mph. For battery-backup systems, this is enough wind to keep the batteries charged and help reduce your electric bill. If you instead opt for a direct grid-tied system, you'll want an annual average wind speed of at least 10 mph.

Turbines: A Quick Look at the Windy Beasts

When home-based wind turbines are discussed, the image conjured up in your mind is probably that of a horizontal-axis machine. Consisting of a propeller, a rotor, a generator, and usually a tail, these turbines resemble wingless aircraft with oversized propellers. Though they may all look somewhat similar from a distance, there's a lot of difference between turbines, and your success or failure as a wind farmer will largely depend on which one you choose. Different machines are designed for different types of wind. Generally, machines with large sweep areas, such as African Wind Power's AWP 3.6 and Southwest Windpower's Whisper 200 (the re-engineered H80), are engineered to operate optimally in lighter winds. Other machines, including the Whisper 100 (the re-engineered H40), have shorter propeller blades and are designed to take the punishment meted out at hilltop locations and during severe storms. Still other turbines, such as the machines produced by Bergey Windpower and Proven Energy, can endure some really nasty weather and still perform well in light winds.

Bergey Windpower's 7.5 to 10 kW Excel tubine. *Photo courtesy of Bergey Windpower.*

Comparing wind turbines apples-for-apples will take a little research. Different machines have different cut-in speeds and different rated wind speeds, which is the speed at which optimal performance is achieved—usually in the 22- to 29-mph range. The table on page 116 lists the rated wind speeds, along with other pertinent data, for a few popular machines. It should be noted that there are many well-built turbines out there that aren't listed in the table. We're not playing favorites; we just wanted to give you a good cross-section for the purpose of comparison.

Practically all turbines on the market today are 3-blade machines. The 3-blade design runs smoother than a 2-blade unit, and will be a little more efficient at converting wind into watts. As a general rule, the blades on smaller or lighter-duty machines are made from polypropylene, while those on heavier machines are epoxy-coated wood or

Electric Wind Turbines versus Water-Pumpers

When you think "wind generator" do you see a multi-bladed water pump as used to dot the Midwest plains? Why aren't big wide multiple blades used on turbines that make electricity? Water pumpers need lots of start-up torque to get things moving, which the large blade area provides. But once the blade is spinning those multiple blades get in each other's air

stream. Decades of careful experimentation have shown that two or three skinny blades will extract the maximum amount of energy from an air stream. Electric generators have almost no start-up resistance. Thus, the design of modern turbines with the minimum of skinny blades.

Photo by LaVone Ewing.

fiberglass. If damaging winds sweep across your site from time to time, you should avoid plastic blades on turbines of 1,000 watts, or more. Trust me; this is the voice of experience talking.

A braking mechanism is also a handy feature, especially if you live in an area with ferocious gusts that could possibly damage your blades, or where ice storms might cover them with a layer of hoarfrost that can throw the system out of balance. With a wind brake—either mechanical or dynamic (electrical)—you can stop the turbine from spinning and wait for the sun the melt the frost or ice.

While the initial shock to your pocketbook will obviously be greater for larger turbines, the ratio of wattage gained for money spent will also be greater. A larger machine will also outlast one or more smaller ones, and a heavy, slow wind turbine will have a longer lifespan than a light, fast one. So, if you're going the way of the wind, buy as much as you can afford. *(For more information on individual machines and the companies that make them, see chapter 11.)*

Towers: Holding Your Turbine Up in the Breeze

Once you have a pretty good idea what size and type of wind turbine will fit your needs, you'll have to figure out how you're going to hold it up in the path of the wind. There are four basic types of towers used by most homeowners: guyed-pipe, guyed-lattice, free-standing lattice, and tubular monopole towers.

Pipe towers are the cheapest, easiest to set up, and probably the most widely-used. Made from sections of standard, off-the-shelf galvanized steel tubing, they are sleek, slim, and as inconspicuous as a tower can be—which isn't very. They are hinged at the base and then erected with the turbine already

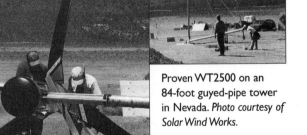

Proven WT2500 on an 84-foot guyed-pipe tower in Nevada. *Photo courtesy of Solar Wind Works.*

Four Tower Types

Guyed Pipe

Guyed Lattice

Free-standing Lattice

Tubular Monopole

A free-standing lattice tower does not need guy wires. *Photo courtesy of Bergey Windpower.*

installed, blades and all. The major drawback to a pipe tower is that you cannot climb it for periodic inspections; it must be lowered.

Guyed-lattice towers are like the old ham radio towers. They are 3-sided and of uniform dimension from top to bottom—mine is around 18 inches per side—and, like pipe towers, must be supported by a series of guy wires. They can be assembled either vertically by sections, or on the ground on a hinged base, and tilted-up into place.

Free-standing lattice towers are broad at the base and taper toward the top, much in the same elegant way as the Eiffel Tower. Though more expensive (and showy) than pipe or guyed-lattice towers, you won't have to worry about clothes-lining yourself on a guy wire whenever you walk near it. Like the guyed-lattice towers, free-standing towers can be built in place, or assembled flat and raised to their vertical position.

A fourth type of free-standing tower, currently being offered by Bergey for their 10 kW turbine, is the tubular monopole tower. These are like the solid, tapered steel towers you see holding communication equipment, or lights high in the air above highway exit ramps. They're expensive and require a crane to erect, but are solid and good-looking, and they take up very little ground space.

Most turbine manufacturers offer tower kits sized for each of their turbines, and those who don't sell the kits will make recommendations on which towers will work best with a particular turbine. Listen to these folks—they know what it takes to hold their machines up in the wind. The lateral thrust put on a turbine in a high wind is mind boggling, and nothing you want to experiment with. You wouldn't put a V-8 in go-cart, would you? Same difference.

But even with good engineering, your tower and its foundation, like any structure, may be subject to regulation by your local building department. This means that you will have to comply with whatever codes are in place, since, unlike an un-permitted workshop tucked inconspicuously away in the trees, it's a bit difficult to erect a tower without anyone noticing.

In any event, there's no substitute for sound engineering, so unless you're an engineer and rigger by trade, you should seek professional assistance to ensure that all goes smoothly.

What Type of Power Do Wind Turbines Produce?

By the nature of their design, all wind turbines initially generate 3-phase alternating current by spinning three pairs of magnets around three coils of wire. On turbines designed for battery-based systems, the AC is rectified into DC, either in the turbine, itself, or within the charge controller. These machines will be configured at the factory for 12-, 24- or 48-volt operation.

Turbines designed for direct grid-tied operation, by contrast, churn out high-voltage DC from the turbine (150 – 350 volts for the Windy Boy 1800U inverter, 250 – 550 volts for the 2500U) that is converted to grid-compatible AC within the inverter. For this reason, direct grid-tied wind systems are more efficient than battery-based systems—up to 94 percent efficient—since there is no energetically-expensive transformation from DC electrical energy, to chemical energy with-in a battery, and back again into electrical energy that must be further converted from DC to AC by the inverter.

How High?
California allows towers of at least 65 feet on any property of one acre or more, and at least 80 feet on 5 acres or larger. Many states still limit tower heights to 35 feet, which severely limits power production.

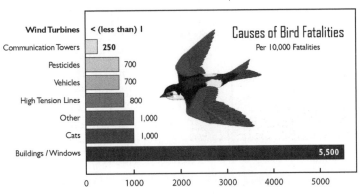

Causes of Bird Fatalities
Per 10,000 Fatalities

Wind Turbines	< (less than) 1
Communication Towers	250
Pesticides	700
Vehicles	700
High Tension Lines	800
Other	1,000
Cats	1,000
Buildings / Windows	5,500

Source: "Summary of Anthropogenic Causes of Bird Mortality," by Erickson et al., 2002. (www.awea.org)

The Power in Wind?

There's more than one way to skin a cat, as the expression goes, and there are various methods used to calculate the power density of the wind, each yielding different results. The common formula – wind power density $(W/m^2) = 0.05472 \times$ wind speed (mph^3) – is a QND (quick & dirty) way to an acceptable result. For the more painstaking methods used by NREL scientists for DOE wind studies, read the Wind Energy Resource Atlas of the United States at *http://rredc.nrel.gov/ wind/pubs/atlas/chp1.html.*

Which System Is Right For Me?

What's true for solar is true for wind. If you live in the backwoods of Minnesota where blizzards and ice storms can tear down power lines in the blink of eye and outages last for days on end, then you'd best be looking for a warm, cozy place to keep your batteries. On the other hand, if you live on the outskirts of a town with reliable grid power, then it might make more sense to opt for the more efficient direct grid-tied system. Component-wise, there is very little difference between solar and wind systems. Wind/battery systems are set up just like solar/battery systems. In fact, many wind charge controllers have additional inputs for a solar array. And for direct grid-tied wind systems, the Windy Boy inverters from SMA America have the same features as the Sunny Boy and other comparable grid-tied solar inverters.

The main difference between solar and wind systems—beyond the obvious, of course—is that wind systems require more thought and more homework, owing to the plethora of different turbines and towers to choose from, as well as the widely-varying wind conditions from site to site. Talk directly with the manufacturers, not just the guy who wants to install the type of wind turbine he just happens to sell. Make the manufacturer convince you that their machine is the one best suited to your needs. Do any of your neighbors have winds systems? Knock on a few doors and deluge the people behind them with questions; they'll be happy to display their vast knowledge about harvesting wind energy. In the end, the more you know before you buy, the more pleased you'll be with the results. ❖

CHAPTER EIGHT
What's It Really Going To Cost Me?

Solar energy is expensive up front, there's no dancing around that fact, so let's face it squarely. You can't really get in the grid-tied door for less than $5,000. The average grid-tie system installed and permitted goes for around $20,000 to $25,000 before rebates or other incentives. Unlike most conventional power sources, solar's expense is all up front. There are almost no operational costs, it doesn't wear out no matter how hard you use it, and there are no long-term societal costs such as air pollution, environmental degradation, or reduced resources for our children. It's like you're buying years of electrical output in advance. All great reasons to feel warm and fuzzy, but it still needs to be affordable today.

Prices Keep Dropping

Photovoltaic prices have declined on average 4% per year over the past 15 years.

We'll base these rule-of-thumb estimates on kilowatt-hours per day. Look at your monthly utility bill. Divide your monthly kWh total use by the number of billing days, usually about 30, to see about how many kWh you're burning per day. The U.S. average is around 20. What would you like to shave yours down to? Remember that your solar system doesn't need to cover all your electric use. Want to cut your electric bill in half? Can do.

What's it going to cost in your case? Based on the actual installed costs we've seen for direct-intertie systems over the past couple years, you can roughly figure on investing about $2,000 for every kilowatt-hour per day you want to shave off your bill.

A Rough Estimate

For a direct-intertie system, you can roughly figure investing $2,000 for every kilowatt-hour per day you want to shave off your utility bill. For battery-based, grid-tied systems, $3,000 per kilowatt-hour per day is within the ballpark.

This is total cost, including installation and permits, but before any rebates, tax credits, or other incentives that will reduce the cost. Battery-based systems span a wider range of costs due to the variable size and quality of the battery bank, but figuring $3,000 per kilowatt-hour per day you want to save is firmly within the ballpark.

Grid-tie systems rarely try to cover your entire electric use. Sure, they could, but that's liable to be frighteningly expensive, and in most utility districts if you make more power over a yearly period than you use, you give the surplus to your friendly local utility company at no charge. Ouch! Nobody likes that prospect. However, most utilities let you carry over a credit from one month to the next within that yearly period. So if you make more power in one month than you use—a likely scenario in summer, or if you're on vacation, or this is a seasonal home—then you can save that credit for use later in the autumn or winter.

A direct-tie system will shave kilowatt-hours off the top of your bill. So those more expensive watt-hours over baseline rates are the first to go. Most homeowners who want to purchase a utility grid-tie system will size their system to deliver about 35 percent to 65 percent of their power use. These systems are very adaptable, because anything the solar doesn't cover gets picked up seamlessly by your existing utility.

Why Don't I See Tracking Mounts?

A tracking mount is one that follows the sun from east to west every day. By facing the modules directly at the sun, daily output can be boosted up to 30% in summer, or 10–15% in winter. Ten years ago trackers were common. Since then, the cost of PV modules has dropped 50%, while tracking mounts have only gotten more expensive. Plus, trackers tend to require regular maintenance, and finally, none of the current rebate programs give extra credit for the expensive tracking mounts. Economics simply don't favor trackers any more. Want more output? Buy another module or two, put 'em on a fixed mount and never think about it again. There's much to be said for *no moving parts!* Except for some specialized pumping systems the era of tracking mounts has pretty much passed.

Real-World Output (what should I really expect?)

Solar sales people will be happy to quote all kinds of confusing numbers at you, such as array wattage, inverter kilowatts, hours of daily sunlight, percent of full sun, etc. Yikes! Want it easy and honest? Here's a simple formula that delivers a fairly accurate, although slightly conservative yearly average output:

(PV Array Wattage) x (Ave. Hours of Sun) x 75% = Daily Watt-Hours

For our example let's assume we have 18 Sharp 165-watt PV modules connected to an SMA Sunny Boy 2500 inverter in the Sacramento, California area. This is a fairly average-size system.

PV Array Wattage is the manufacturer's label rating: in this case, 165 watts times 18 modules = 2,970 watts.

Average Hours of Sun is a yearly average of noontime-equivalent hours. This ranges from 4.0 to 5.5 hours for most of the U.S. The National Renewable Energy Lab monitored hundreds of sites from 1960 thru 1990, and then distilled it down very nicely in their Redbook. You can download individual states or the whole thing in pdf format at: *http://rredc.nrel.gov/solar/pubs/redbook/*.

The Sacramento page tells us that a south-facing, fixed array mounted at latitude angle (38°), or at latitude minus 15° (38°–15°= 23°) will receive 5.5 hours of noontime equivalent sun every day on a yearly average. Twenty-three degrees just happens to be about the same angle as typical 4:12 or 5:12 suburban roofs.

A fudge factor of **75 percent** takes into account all the real-world effects of dirty modules, dirty air,

A California home sports a 3.0 kW solar array comprised of 18 Sharp 165-watt modules and an SMA Sunny Boy 2,500-watt inverter. *Photo courtesy of Real Goods.*

Is It Going To Get Cheaper If I Wait?

Thanks to mass production, improved installation techniques, and smarter installers, the cost of solar has been gradually coming down. PV is about 50% cheaper now than it was 10 years ago. On the flip side, every rebate program has tended to be better funded and more generous initially. As interest grows, rebates are usually diluted to cover more systems. The decision is yours.

high humidity, hot modules, wiring losses, small bits of shading, inverter inefficiency, and all the other little things that are less than laboratory perfect in a working system. For battery-based systems, a factor of 70 percent is closer to reality. If your array is perfectly shade-free, installed perfectly, and you're in a dry climate above 6,000 feet elevation (and your karma is really good), then bump the factor up an extra 3-4 percent.

So our example will be: 2,970 watts x 5.5 hours x 0.75 = 12,251 watt-hours or 12.25 kWh per day. Remember, this is a yearly average. Most folks will see about twice as much power production in the summer, as in the winter.

So long as there are no serious shading or other performance-reducing site problems, this formula usually yields a conservative estimate. Most customers report slightly better performance with their actual installed systems. Better to look like a hero than a bum has always been my goal, and you certainly can't depend on the weather to be the same every year, even in California. The long term Redbook charts state, "Uncertainty ± 9 percent." Take your result as a very educated guesstimate...your mileage may vary...but probably not more than 5 percent. ❖

A home in New Jersey was retrofit with 2.7 kW of Evergreen solar panels. *Photo courtesy of Evergreen Solar.*

CHAPTER NINE
Yikes! Any Financial Help Out There?

Yes, solar is expensive initially, but help is on the way. There are a wide variety of rebates, grants, buydown programs, tax credits, and exemptions available. But there are no blanket rules. Every state is different. How much help you'll be able to round up to pay for your particular system varies regionally. Some of these programs will cover 50 percent or even more of a complete system installed cost. There is, as of yet, little Federal encouragement of solar investments at the residential level, but there are a wide variety of individual state and sometimes individual city or utility companies that are offering assistance. The best place to start looking is at the Database of State Incentives for Renewable Energy (DSIRE) *www.dsireusa.org*. Established in 1995, DSIRE is an ongoing project of the Interstate Renewable Energy Council (IREC), funded by the U.S. Department of Energy and managed by the North Carolina Solar Center with support from the University of North Carolina. DSIRE has a vast wealth of well-organized information. It's the best info source to check first. Their info is accurate, and updated weekly. They'll give you bullet points, a written summary, and access info for each program. There isn't much that escapes their notice, except perhaps small, local programs. There are a few small city-based programs it doesn't list, but that brings us to your next level of potential financing help.

Financial Help?

The best place to start looking is the Database of State Incentives for Renewable Energy **www.dsireusa.org**

Local Sources

You second source of help will be local installers. These are the folks who will know about local assistance programs. Anyone who's working locally doing any kind of solar energy installations will be well-aware of any financial incentives that are available to their potential customers, and will be downright eager for you to hear about them. Start by looking in your local Yellow Pages under *SOLAR*. Next, in our appendix you'll find a full listing of the state energy offices for every U.S. state. Very often they will have listings of businesses offering solar services and installations. The amount of help your state energy office can offer will vary greatly, depending on whether your state is actively promoting renewable energy or not. In California you'll find lots of solar help; in North Dakota you'll do better to ask about wind energy.

If you're fortunate enough to be in a state with an active rebate program you'll probably find you've got a choice of local installers. Lucky you. Shop around. Prices and services vary widely. Ask dealers for local job references. Any reputable dealer should have a string of happy customers they're pleased to share with you. Some installation companies are willing to do some or all of the paper wrangling for rebates, permits, permissions, etc. in return for your business. This is no small favor. The learning curve on these forms is steep, and the time required isn't slight. Knowing how to deal effectively with the many bureaucracies involved can save you major frustrations and delays. If you have a licensed installer who's also willing to handle the paperwork, count yourself blessed! Some companies may even offer to accept the State rebate in lieu of payment

A fully solar-fitted home with black pool-heating panels, a large PV array, and a domestic hot water collector at the far end, this homeowner is set to enjoy a lifetime of low energy bills. *Photo courtesy of Shell Solar.*

from you. Those are dollars that never need to leave your pocket, and since the installer can't claim the rebate until your installation is finished and signed off, you're assured of a speedy, code-compliant install.

Cheap Money

Financial trends lately have run toward low interest rates, escalating real estate values, and rising energy costs. You can turn this to your advantage by borrowing against the equity of your home, often at surprisingly low interest rates, and that interest is then tax-deductible. Use this cash to pay for your solar/wind electric system. Many homeowners have found that the savings on their electric bills are greater than their payments on a long-term equity loan. Your system actually pays for itself thanks to lower bills. Higher electric rates and lower interest rates obviously favor this scenario. The best payoff happens when your electric bill regularly exceeds the lowest-cost baseline rates. Plus, you've insulated yourself against future rate hikes, and while the loan pays off in 15 years or so, your RE system keeps delivering dependably for decades.

Installing a solar electric system increases the value of your home, particularly as Americans continue to become more energy conscious. According to a now somewhat dated, but extensively researched study from the National Appraisal Institute (*Appraisal Journal,* Oct. 1999), your home's value increases $20 for every $1 reduction in annual utility bills. This is a ratio that will only increase as energy costs rise. At 1999 rates, a modest solar electric system of 2,500 watts will increase your home's value by $8,000 to $10,000 immediately just for the utility bill reduction. Many states have adopted property tax exemption laws, such that if your home value is increased by a solar installation, you cannot be taxed on that increased value. You'll find details at the DSIRE website.

Whose Green Tags are These?

Green Tags are a commodity that can be traded and sold (see next page), but there's controversy over who owns them. California utility giants are claiming they own the tags; most other states have laws that specifically give the tags to the homeowner. Until the courts decide, California homeowners are out of luck.

Renewable Energy Credits or Green Tags

If your solar or wind electric system is providing renewably-generated energy, not only do you get an immediate reduction in your utility bill, but you are creating a commodity called Renewable Energy Credits, or Green Tags. These represent the environmental benefits of your clean energy separated, or unbundled, from the actual kilowatt-hours of energy. In most states these credits can be sold or traded like any commodity. Essentially, you're selling the bragging rights to your green power, but not the actual power.

It works like this, say some major corporation wants to paint a greener image of themselves (no really, it happens sometimes!). Rather than invest big bucks in their own solar electric system, Mega-Bucks Inc. buys up the green tags from a number of smaller systems that a broker has assembled. Now Mega-Bucks can legally say, "We get X percentage of our energy from renewable sources, we are soooooo good you should just run out right now and buy all our products!" Once you've sold your green tags, you can no longer say that you get your energy from a renewable source, even though you certainly continue to in reality. You can say that you're hosting a solar energy array, and you can point to it and say, "See the nifty solar array on my house? It makes an average of 20 kWh per day!" You just can't claim the environmental benefits. But then you've got some extra bucks in your pocket that you can claim. Credits vary depending mostly on the size of your system. Most residential systems are currently worth $50 to $500 per year for the green tags, and you can continue to sell your credits (or not) on a yearly basis. ❖

Working around shade problems. The chimney, and the shade it casts in the afternoon, cost space for three modules on this rooftop. Since it didn't seem likely they'd move the chimney, the system designer had to work around it. Still, seventeen modules (2,975 watts) is a very nice-sized array for moderately conservative homeowners. *Photo courtesy of Affinity Energy, Windsor, CA.*

CHAPTER TEN

Permits and Paperwork

Paperwork. It's nobody's favorite thing to deal with, but we've got some tips, suggestions, and hard-won experience that can make it less of an ordeal.

What to Expect

Because we're writing this book for homeowners from Seattle to Miami, we can only generalize about the particular forms you may need for your installation, but we've found there are at least three forms you can count on:

1. State or local government programs are going to have some forms to complete if you expect to cash-in on a rebate, grant, buy-down, or however they've structured it. In most cases you need to be pre-approved, so this is generally the first form to file. After approval, your funds are put in escrow, and you've got a reasonable amount of time to install the system, typically six to twelve months, then come back to claim your dollars.

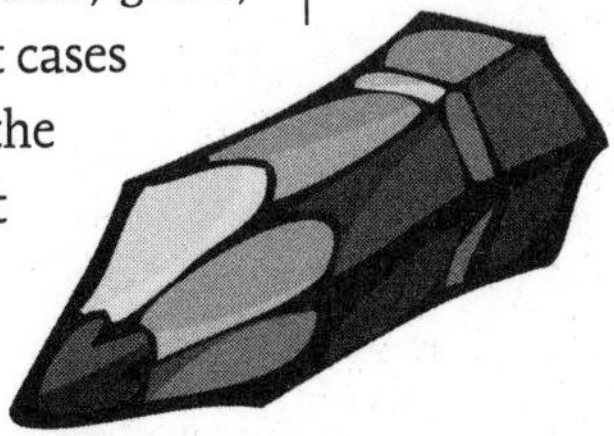

2. A local building permit from your city or county is a necessity, and typically the rebate folks will want a copy of this when it's

Luminous Abundance

The earth receives more energy from the sun in just one hour than the world uses in a whole year.

Source: SolarBuzz.com

signed off as proof that the installation actually happened, and it was done to comply with building and electric codes.

3. In order to correctly setup billing and credit, and record your home on their distributed generation maps, the local utility company will have their own set of forms, and sometimes an inspection. They usually require a signed-off building permit submitted with their forms, so this is probably the last process that needs attention.

Find Somebody Else To Do It!

For those who really hate paperwork, our first tip is a slice of heaven. Let somebody else do all the paper wrangling! This isn't as far-fetched as it might sound. If you're in a state with a good, active rebate program there are likely to be several contractors or installation firms that want your business. One of the ways they can get it is by handling most or all of the paper hassles. As someone who has been in this business since the beginning, and has wrangled more than his share of rebate paperwork, take my word... this is a great incentive when you can find it! Even for pros who know exactly what's required by which bureaucracy, this service probably represents at least eight to twelve hours of someone's time in the background. And that's if Murphy's Law doesn't rear its head, and everything goes smoothly with no "lost" paperwork or misunderstandings. Be prepared to pay a bit extra for this kind of service...and then feel good and smug about it.

A California home with a 3.0 kW grid-tied system (18 Sharp 165-watt modules and one SMA Sunny Boy 2,500-watt inverter). *Photo courtesy of Real Goods.*

Do It Yourself?

Feel like you can handle this yourself? Good for you! But first a warning about doing the physical hardware installation yourself. Most of the big rebate programs have a self-installed penalty clause. In California and New Jersey it's a 15 percent reduction in your available rebate. They'd rather not have contractors and industry insiders using up all the funds, for obvious reasons. So even if you are a contractor, and you really are buying this system for your own house, you might want to hire a fellow contractor to sell and install it for you. With the extra 15 percent rebate you can afford it, and it'll probably ease the paperwork hassles a bit.

Now, as to doing the paperwork yourself, all the major programs have forms and guide books for filling them out available online. Just download and go for it. Be sure to fill in ALL the info. If you aren't sure what they want, call them. These programs are heavily subscribed to, and it sometimes takes three or four months for them to process your paperwork. To have forms returned because of missing info— three months later—is discouraging, to say the least.

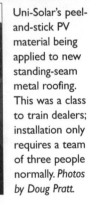

Uni-Solar's peel-and-stick PV material being applied to new standing-seam metal roofing. This was a class to train dealers; installation only requires a team of three people normally. *Photos by Doug Pratt.*

Don't fax, FedEx. Another tip born of experience. Although most of these agencies give you a fax number, we've found that the occasional unreadable item—that doesn't get noticed and returned till three months later—makes the extra $10 for express delivering the originals seem like a bargain. FedEx or UPS also gives you proof-positive of precisely when an application arrived. Handy proof to have when an application gets "lost."

Keep copies of everything! This is very important, and has pulled my bacon out of the fire more than a few times. The agencies doing solar rebates are big, busy, oversubscribed, and understaffed. Stuff gets lost, gets misrouted, who knows? Having copies of everything you submitted is a must. Hopefully you'll never need them. But when you do need them, you'll need them BAD! In a worst case this can save you from having to start all over at the end of the line.

Tell Your Friendly Local Utility Company

Typical system being installed, with a Sunny Boy 2500 inverter in the center (cover off for wiring), a DC disconnect on the right, and an AC disconnect on the left. Far left is the existing house meter and main breaker panel, also with the cover removed for ease of wiring. *Photo by Doug Pratt.*

Your grid-tie system will function perfectly whether your utility company knows about it and has given their official blessing or not. Hardware is funny like that. In fact, your installer should turn it on briefly just to check that everything is functioning correctly at the end of the installation. But briefly to check performance is all that it should be on until the utility company does their inspection (if required), and gives permission to start intertie. The utility companies take unpermitted power input very seriously. Get caught pushing your meter backwards without permission and you can very easily find yourself locked off from grid power, and facing some stiff fines.

So fill out the utility company paperwork. Besides getting yourself the right to spin your meter backwards legally, this will get you on their local mapping so that repair crews know you're a potential generator. It also ensures that you've got the correct type of meter installed. The standard clockwork type meters will spin forward or backward just fine, but the one you've got now was only certified to be accurate going forward. They'll probably install a new bi-directional meter for you. You may have some choices about what kind of billing program you're going to be on. If your house is usually empty during the day, you may want to consider Time-of-Use billing, if it's available for you (read on).

Sell High, Buy Low

That old stock market saw has a new meaning in the California utility intertie market. The state legislature has ruled that any billing scheme normally available to a homeowner, has to continue to be available to them if they install a solar electric system. This means that Time-of-Use (TOU) billing is available to solar grid-tie homeowners. The idea behind TOU was to reduce electric demand on weekday summer afternoons by raising rates between noon and 6:00 p.m. Now solar homeowners can sell kilowatt hours for about 32 cents in the afternoon, and buy them back for about 9 cents in the evening. It's legal, and the credit shows up as dollars on your bill. This has naturally become very popular with grid-tie system owners, because it will speed your payback by 15 to 40 percent for most households. Time-of-Use favors the typical modern household where everyone's off to work or school most of the afternoon. You want to be sure to schedule electric chores before noon or after six, as much as practical. Pool pumps and air conditioning are good candidates for rescheduling. TOU billing has a summer schedule, May through October, when there's a large differential between peak and off-peak rates, which just happens to largely coincide with peak solar output in most locations. There's a much smaller rate offset the rest of the year, currently about 12 cents and 10 cents, but you still get to sell in the afternoon at a slightly higher rate than you buy back in the evening.

Ground-mounted arrays (15 kW of solar power) supply a grid-tied home outside Albany, New York. *Photo courtesy of Global Resource Options, White River Junction, VT.*

U.S. Wind Power

At the end of 2004, approximately 6,740 megawatts of utility-scale wind installations were operating in 30 states across the U.S., plus another 2,000 megawatts in the planning stages. This does not include the tens of thousands of small wind turbines used directly by homeowners.

Now Comes the Good Part...

Once your utility representative has inspected and given their blessing, you're free to let those high-powered solar-generated electrons rip. Turn the system on and enjoy watching that meter spin backwards. If you make more energy than you use in a month you'll probably find a credit on your bill. Every state, and sometimes every utility company within a state, has their own rules for how to deal with credits. The most common scenario allows you to roll credits forward from month to month for a 12-month period. If you end the year with credit still on the books you'll probably give it away, although some utilities will pay you their wholesale price, and others simply cash you out at wholesale rates every month. Make sure you understand how your utility deals with credits, because you can adjust your lifestyle to some degree. Invite all your friends with electric vehicles to come over for instance, or crank up your hydrogen electrolyzer, or I've even heard stories about some kinds of agricultural pursuits and grow lights. If you've got extra, you'll find a creative way to use it.

Don't Get Too Smug About It

A small word of warning is needed at this point. I've known some folks with modest grid-tie systems that ended up with a higher electric bill after they turned their system on. No, it was working perfectly. The inverter's built-in cumulative watt-hour meter showed their system was actually delivering slightly more energy than predicted. It was a mental attitude thing. "Oh we've got solar power now, we don't need to worry about turning the lights off." In the energy conservation biz we called this "take back" and it's common. "Oh, I've got solar hot water, so I can hang out in the shower a few minutes longer without feeling guilty." We all do it, it's human nature. Just be aware you're doing it, and don't whine about the results. ❖

CHAPTER ELEVEN

The Nuts and Bolts: What To Look For, What To Avoid

Okay, you've decided that solar or wind energy seems like a good idea, and now you're shopping for the right bits and pieces for your system. This chapter is where you get to tap our many years of experience with good, bad, and indifferent solar equipment manufacturers. I've always believed that honesty was the best sales tool, and, so much as editors and lawyers allow, you'll find real-world honest assessments here.

Solar Modules

Close to 80 percent of your investment is probably going to go into PV modules, so your choice matters...or does it? The good news is that module quality is universally excellent. You should expect a product with a 20- to 25-year performance warranty, and regardless of manufacturer, you'll enjoy long, trouble-free ownership. The bad news is that solar energy has become immensely popular around the world, and since 2003 there has been a worldwide shortage of solar panels. So whatever brand and wattage of PV modules your dealer can actually deliver is a good brand. They'll be fine. Generally bigger is better. PV modules are sold by how many watts they deliver under a standardized test. With higher-wattage modules you don't need

Good News!

Your biggest investment in a solar electric system – the solar modules – have the best warranties... 20 to 25 years.

as many, which results in less bolting and wiring. Most power production modules are in the 100- to 200-watt range now. All that being said, there are a few other fine points to consider in module selection.

Single or Poly-Crystalline Solar Modules

On average, you're going to get 10-12 watts of output for every square foot of area with single or polycrystalline modules. With typical U.S. sun of 5 hours per day, that square foot will deliver about 50 watt-hours every day on a yearly average. Let's look at a few modules:

BP 160 or 170 watts	62.7" x 31.1" = 13.5 sq. ft.	(1.25 m²)	12.2 watts/sq. ft.
Evergreen Cedar-Series 115 watts	62.4" x 25.7" = 11.1 sq. ft.	(1.03 m²)	10.3 watts/sq. ft.
Kyocera 167 watts	50.8" x 39" = 13.7 sq. ft.	(1.27 m²)	12.1 watts/sq. ft.
Sharp 165 or 175 watts	62" x 32.5" = 13.99 sq. ft.	(1.30 m²)	12.1 watts/sq. ft.
Shell PowerMax Ultra 165 or 175 watts	64" x 32" = 14.2 sq. ft.	(1.32 m²)	12.0 watts/sq. ft.

Amorphous Modules

Uni-Solar ECO-series 124 watts	96.8" x 31.2" = 20.9 sq. ft.	(1.94 m²)	5.9 watts/sq. ft.

PV Connections

PV modules are equipped with either junction boxes (J-box) with a terminal strip inside, or with Multi-Contact cables, usually just called "MC cables." Some module brands are showing up with both. If you don't need the MC cables, you simply disconnect them inside the J-box. MC cables have become the preferred connector for direct grid-tied systems, where we need to make a lot of series connections. The MC connectors just plug together in series, making module wiring very fast and fool proof. J-box modules are usually preferred for battery-based systems, which use less, or sometimes no series connections at all.

In either case, don't pass up a batch of available modules just because they don't have the optimum connector type. This is just a matter of convenience. Either connector type will function okay with any installation. In the worst case, you or your installer might spend an extra couple hours on wiring.

Be sure that when the installation is finished, any extra MC cabling is secured neatly under the modules and isn't laying on the roof surface. Twenty years of the wind blowing a cable back and forth across an asphalt shingle will wear it down to nothing, exposing the high-voltage wiring. Cables can be secured with zip ties, although even in the shade, the life expectancy of the zip tie is far less than your modules. Quality installations use galvanized spring steel clips or just short pieces of twisted wire to secure the cabling.

Uni-Solar's unique thin-film solar modules are nearly invisible when applied to conventional charcoal-grey metal roofing (arrows point to the solar roof), as shown on this 1.5 kW Research Townhome by the National Association of Home Builders. *Photo courtesy of UNI-SOLAR.*

Amorphous modules are slightly better in low-light, may have a big advantage in partial shading, experience less voltage drop at higher temperatures, but need 30 to 50 percent more space for mounting.

Module Construction

Single-crystal and polycrystalline modules with full-perimeter aluminum frames and tempered glass covers are the norm, and will deliver the most wattage with the least surface area. Amorphous silicon modules require about 50 percent more surface area to collect the same amount of wattage, but can be built without glass covers for an unbreakable module. Uni-Solar® offers a couple unique amorphous products designed to be the roof, not just sit on it. They have a shingle product that interweaves with conventional asphalt shingles, or a peel-and-stick product for application on standing-seam metal roof pans. (It's greatly preferred to do application on new pans, before they're installed.) Both these products are vandal- and theft-proof, and are slightly more expensive than conventional modules.

Module Mounting Systems

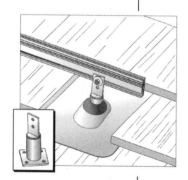

A typical standoff, flashing, and rail assembly. Each row of PV modules will have a pair of rails under them. *Drawing courtesy of UniRac.*

Mounting technology has advanced by leaps and bounds the past few years. The standard system now is made of extruded aluminum rails in various pre-cut lengths with slots top and bottom that permit adjustment for various module sizes and rafter spans. Tilt-up leg hardware is added as needed.

Attachment to the roof is usually done with standoffs, which penetrate the roofing, and are waterproofed with a flashing just like a plumbing vent (which every roofer understands). With conventional asphalt shingles, the more expensive standoffs are optional, and are not absolutely required. With shake or tile roofs, standoffs are required. *(See photos on pages 62 and 128.)*

Ground-mounted PV arrays use the same rail mounting systems; we just add legs for small arrays, or more commonly, an engineered pipe framework for larger modules *(see photos below and page 91).* Poletop mounts hang the array from the top of a single steel pipe, around 4- to 6-inch in diameter. These pole-mounted arrays are less popular for grid-tied systems because we can't usually hang more than about 10 modules on a single pole due to wind loading, and grid-tied systems often run 20 to 60 modules.

UniRac *(www.unirac.com)* and Direct Power and Water *(www.directpower.com)* both make quality mounting systems.

Spanish, or barrel tile, is a special case. Just stay off it if there's anyplace else to put your array! It's difficult and expensive to work with. If the roof is truly the only place, then Professional Solar Products *(www.pro solar.com)* makes Tile Trac®, the best mounting hardware package for Spanish tile. It puts no weight on the tile, attaches securely to the rafter, and still manages to penetrate the tile at its highest point so there's little chance of leakage. It doesn't make tile mounting fast or fun, but does make it possible.

TOP: The back side of a pole-mounted solar array shows UniRac's mounting system and the black junction boxes of the solar panels. *Photo courtesy of UniRac.*

LEFT: The mounting system for 20 Kyocera 158-watt panels, installed on the Grove dance club, along with two PV Powered inverters. *Photo courtesy of Sunlight Solar Energy, Bend, Oregon.*

Direct Grid-Tie Inverters

Now here you've got some choices! There's a wealth of good inverters on the market now, with more showing up every few months, and there's no lack of stock. Your dealer should be able to get you any model you want with no problem. Your inverter will come with at least a five-year manufacturer's warranty, because the rebate programs say they have to. *(The most popular models are listed alphabetically below.)*

Fronius IG-series Inverters

www.fronius.com/worldwide/usa.solarelectronics/

Fronius is an Austrian company with roots in DC welding and battery-charging technology. Thanks to the German solar market they've been producing grid-tie inverters since 1995, so there's some experience here, although their entry into the U.S. market didn't start until

Fronius IG3000 inverter.
Photo courtesy of Fronius.

2004. Offering U.S. residential models at 2,000, 3,000, 4,000, and 5,100 watts, Fronius has several unique features. Using small, powerful, high-frequency transformers, the weight is dramatically reduced (42 pounds vs. a similar capacity competitor at 130 pounds), and adaptability is increased. Long-life fans are used at proportional speeds when extra cooling is required. Fan life expectancy exceeds 15 years if run 24/7. The built-in software is extremely fast at finding the maximum power point under changing conditions, so they'll extract the maximum possible energy. They have simple expansion slots like a computer for easily adding remote monitoring, environment sensing, or other future improvements. Their power boards are completely dipped in conformal coating for the greatest resistance to moisture and corrosion. Most manufacturers just coat the back of the board. If you're in a humid environment, this could mean a much longer life expectancy. The NEMA 3R housing is okay for indoor or outdoor mounting. The Fronius inverter also has a nice full-featured LCD display, easy mounting, quick wiring connections, and they're FCC compliant for greatly reduced radio/TV noise. Setting up an optional remote computer display is quick and simple, with standard Ethernet connections. Their larger 4,000 to 5,100 watt units have two power channels. When incoming power is lower, only one channel operates, which gives slightly better efficiency. The "master" channels alternate automatically every other day. Altogether, Fronius makes impressive inverters that typically retail from a bit under, to a bit over $1/watt. Larger sizes are more cost effective.

PV Powered Inverters   *www.pvpowered.com*

PV Powered is an Oregon-based company. (Yes, Oregon is part of the U.S. the last time anyone checked.) They are a more recent addition to the field, so they don't have an extensive track record, but they are the only manufacturer with a standard 10-year warranty. Designed on the KISS principle (Keep It Simple Stupid), PV Powered inverters have by far the lowest number of parts of any inverter on the market. Fewer parts means less chance of something failing, thus the longer warranty and the expectation that this should be a very dependable, long-lived inverter. PV Powered currently offers models at 1,800 and 2,800 watts. A larger model near 4,000 watts is under development and may be available by the time you read this. Thanks to extremely high efficiency, an oversize heat sink, and good thermal design,

PV Powered 2800 inverter. *Photo courtesy of PV Powered.*

NEMA? What's a NEMA?

NEMA is the National Electrical Manufacturers Association. They provide industry-standard ratings for electrical equipment, as in what sort of protection the housing on your electric gizmo offers, or what kind of environment it can be installed in. Higher numbers generally denote more protection. The most common ratings are:

◆ **NEMA 1**: the most basic rating to keep little fingers out, for indoor use only.

◆ **NEMA 2**: for indoor use only, but with added protection from dripping or light splashing of liquids.

◆ **NEMA 3**: for indoor or outdoor use, provides protection against rain, snow, sleet, falling dirt, or windblown dust.

◆ **NEMA 3R**: same as NEMA 3, but without protection from windblown dust. (Probably due to ventilation slots.)

◆ **NEMA 4**: same as NEMA 3, but with added protection from hose- or sprinkler-directed water streams. (No ventilation slots, probably watertight sealed.)

NEMA 4 is typically the highest rating we'll find on any household electric equipment. But just so you'll know, NEMA 4X adds corrosion protection (used in the marine industry), NEMA 6 adds brief submersion, and NEMA 7 is for explosive environments.

PV Powered inverters run cooler, don't require a fan, and don't require any power limiting software features at higher temperatures. They simply won't get hot. The current models haven't been FCC tested, and some radio noise problems have been reported. New models will be FCC compliant. The NEMA 3R enclosure is approved for indoor or outdoor mounting. An inverter-mounted fluorescent display is standard, and the serial connection for remote monitoring is included with all models. The computer software is a free download, and PV Powered inverters are usually competitively priced at under $1/watt.

Sharp SunVista Inverter   *http://solar.sharpusa.com*
Sharp is a Japanese-based company with extensive production facilities in the United States. (They produce PV modules in Tennessee for the U.S. market.) The SunVista inverter is made in Japan, and has a large installed base with an excellent track record both in Japan and

Inverters You Don't Want

Let's take a moment to mention some inverters you don't want. It's unlikely you'll run into either of these unless you're shopping for used equipment, but just in case…

AES (Advanced Energy Systems) GC-1000. Many of these relatively small 1000-watt inverters were installed until about 2002 when this particular U.S.-based AES went belly up. (There's a different AES out of Australia now; a completely different company.) They don't seem to have a particularly long-life expectancy, and there's no repair or warranty service available. Warranties are only as good as the companies that issue them. You don't want a GC-1000 unless it's free! (And even then it's iffy.)

Trace/Xantrex Sun-Tie Series This was the first mass-produced, direct-intertie inverter on the market. You may still find a few of these for sale cheap. They were rushed to market and suffered a wide variety of problems. Xantrex had just bought Trace, and while getting settled, had some trouble admitting any faults. Eventually they genuinely tried hard to make good. By then the bad reputation had caught hold and it was like trying to sell return tickets for the Titanic's maiden voyage. They couldn't give them away. Better to stay away from this discontinued model.

the U.S. The 3,500 watt SunVista is actually three smaller inverters in a single box. This unique construction allows for three different PV arrays. The arrays can all be the same, or each can point in a different direction, with different numbers (or even brands and wattages) of modules. For homes with limited space this option makes system design much easier. Fit what you can on the southface, then add on to the east and/or west as needed. Each array is MPPT-tracked individually, extracting the maximum energy that particular array can manage. Cooling, if required, is by proportional fans. The NEMA 3R enclosure is okay for indoor or outdoor mounting, and is an easy-to-live-with beige color. A remote display is included that shows instantaneous output, cumulative output for the past year, and total CO_2 abatement since installation...good for bragging rights. The SunVista is FCC compliant. This is a good solid inverter with very few problem reports. It usually sells for right around $1/watt.

SMA Sunny Boy and Windy Boy Inverters

www.sma-america.com

SMA of Germany makes Sunny Boy inverters. They have been producing inverters in Germany for the European market since the mid-1990s, so there's some considerable experience and a wide range of models here. Sunny Boy America offers models at 700, 1,100, 1,800, 2,500, and 6,000 watts. The Sunny Boy 2500 is undoubtedly the most popular grid-tie inverter in America. They had the great good fortune to show up just about the time everybody was figuring out what a lemon the first-generation Xantrex Sun-Tie was, and enjoyed an enthusiastic welcome from installers that still hasn't entirely worn off. They feature powder-coated, stainless-steel, completely sealed, NEMA 4-rated enclosures that prefer to be mounted outdoors in a shady location, or at least not in the sun on south- or west-facing walls. Indoor installations will

Sharp's SunVista inverter and display. *Photo courtesy of Sharp.*

require the optional Sunny Breeze temperature-controlled fan that sits on top of the heat sink. The stock color is RED! Yes, they're *very* red, which is a delight to some folks, and a horror to others. Dealers can get toned-down blue or white covers for most models, although this might cost extra. Their MPPT software is solid, and there have been few problems with this brand. The inverter-mounted display, formerly an extra-cost option, is now standard equipment. It shows instant wattage, cumulative for the day, cumulative since installation, voltage of the array, a few other readings, and any error codes. Remote or multiple inverter monitoring, either locally or web-based, is available as an option. All SMA inverters are FCC-compliant for low radio noise. Sunny Boy inverters usually sell for a slightly-premium price ranging from $1 to over $2/watt. Larger sizes are more cost effective.

Sunny Boy inverter. *Photo courtesy of SMA-America.*

SMA is also the source of the only UL1741 certified inverter for wind turbines. The 1,800- and 2,500-watt models are available under the (what else?) Windy Boy label. Because the Windy Boy software has to be configured to work with a particular brand and size of wind turbine, you'll find this inverter is only offered as a package of turbine and Windy Boy together. There will also be some other control hardware to keep things in check should the utility fail during a windy period. (Power goes out when the wind blows? Gee, really?) For more information, read chapter 7.

Wind Turbines for the Windy Boy

Which turbine manufacturers produce models compatible with SMA America's Windy Boy inverter? Currently the African Wind Power AWP 3.6 (1.5 kW) and AWP 7.2 (7.5 kW) turbines can be configured to work with the Windy Boy, as well as all of the Proven Energy machines above the WT600 (the small 0.6 kW) model. Southwest Windpower's Whisper 200 (1.0 kW) can likewise be adapted. Others will surely follow. Because of the widely varying electrical characteristics of different machines, the Windy Boy inverter must be configured at the factory for your specific model of wind turbine.

SMA has also introduced a unique battery-based inverter that interacts with and supports off-grid or emergency use of their conventional direct-intertie units. We cover the Sunny Island with battery-based inverters below.

Xantrex GT 3.0 Inverter   *www.xantrex.com*

The GT 3.0 is Xantrex's second-generation direct grid-tie inverter, engineered in the U.S. and Canada, and built in China. Xantrex learned their lesson from the problematic first-generation SunTie. They started by asking dealers and installers what they wanted, and then built it. The resulting model was extensively and heavily laboratory tested, and then extensively beta tested out in the real world with experienced PV installers and dealers. It appears they got it right. Everyone who's installed or purchased this relatively new 3,000-watt model has good things to say about it, and the pricing is certainly attractive. Perhaps the nicest feature is the code-compliant, built-in single-knob AC and DC disconnect. Every other inverter on the market requires a separate DC disconnect box to provide de-powered wiring to the inverter (in case the inverter needs to be removed for service). On the GT 3.0, the upper inverter section will separate from the lower disconnect section with no exposed high voltage wiring. Fewer boxes hanging on the wall makes a more attractive installation. No fans are required for cooling, except in extremely hot climates or unshaded south-facing installations. A fan option is available. A nice, fully-featured LCD display is included, as is Ethernet or RS-232 connections for computer monitoring. It's FCC-compliant, so radio noise or interference shouldn't be a problem. The NEMA 3R enclosure is okay for indoor or outdoor installations, and is an agreeable (if perhaps boring) beige color. The GT 3.0 is attractively priced at under $1/watt.

Xantrex's GT 3.0 grid-tie inverter. *Photo courtesy of Xantrex.*

Battery-Based Grid-Tie Inverters

Battery-based systems haven't been as popular as direct-tie, but if your utility power is subject to interruptions due to hurricanes, ice storms, or Enron traders getting rich, then battery-backup is your ticket to security. Your list of choices is shorter and simpler, and here are a few of your options *(listed alphabetically)*.

Beacon's inverter for battery-based systems. *Photo courtesy of Beacon Power.*

Beacon Power   *www.beaconpower.com*

The Beacon Power M5 is a U.S.-made 5,000-watt inverter with an advanced 3-channel MPPT charge controller, switchgear, and ground fault protection all housed in a single NEMA 3R indoor/outdoor box. It offers instant 120VAC backup power and requires minimal space. Batteries, battery housing, and battery overcurrent protection are sold separately, as battery sizing requirements vary. Although it initially seems expensive with a suggested retail just under $7,000, if you need close to 5,000 watts of grid-tie power with battery backup, this is your lowest-cost option, and it certainly takes the least space. The M5 was extensively beta-tested, and has come up clean and trouble-free. Wiring access is easy and roomy for quick installations. Standard monitoring is very minimal...three LEDs that show if anything is abnormal, which may suit non-technical types. If you want more, there's a very good optional PC-based software package with simple plug-in connections.

What doesn't come with the Beacon is an AC-powered battery charger or a generator input. The batteries are only charged by photovoltaics, so once you've depleted the batteries, pray for sun! Generator power can be added with a conventional transfer switch, just like you'd do without the Beacon M5. There's no generator wiring provision or internal transfer switch, as other inverters in this class provide. Also, there's no stacking ability for multiple inverters or

240-volt output (not that you should be running any 240-volt appliances on backup power anyway). Dual M5 units can be installed, and during a utility outage each will deliver an independent 120VAC source. They just won't deliver a 240VAC source between them. The Beacon M5 retails for around $1.40/watt, not including batteries.

Outback Power Systems   *www.outbackpower.com*

Outback was formed when Xantrex bought Trace Engineering around 2000 – 2001, and much of the original Trace engineering staff left for greener fields. Outback's engineering staff has a great wealth of residential inverter experience. They produce four U.S.-made grid-tie models with 2,500 to 3,600 watts continuous output. All models can be stacked for 120/240VAC output at double the wattage. Because this is an engineer-owned company, there are a great variety of options, adjustments, and configurations. (*Leave No Possibility Behind* must be the engineer's creed.) Although all the individual bits and pieces can be purchased separately and assembled on-site, most Outback systems are delivered as pre-assembled and pre-wired Power Centers with a UL label on the assembly that makes electrical inspectors happy. This greatly speeds installation, inspection, and delivers compact packages that are more aesthetically pleasing. Power Centers are approximately 44" wide x 20" high x 13" deep, and weigh 145 pounds with one inverter, or 215 pounds with two inverters.

Outback's pre-assembled PS2 Power Centers are available with one or two inverters. *Photo courtesy of Outback Power Systems.*

Exception to the Rule

Every rule has its exception, and for the rule that all components for a battery-based solar system must be located inside a building, the exception is the OutBack PS1 Power Center—a rainproof, fully-sealed enclosure, containing a GVFX3648 inverter, an MX60 MPPT charge controller, and a quartet of sealed AGM batteries (not included). See *photo on the next page.*

Outback inverters have quickly become the standard for battery-based inverters with a clean, strong waveform, a solid, trouble-free design, and great customer support. Their grid-tied Power Center packages include the awesome Outback MPPT 60-amp charge control with special monitoring software for grid-tie that tracks instant, daily, and cumulative power generation.

Outback inverters will automatically sense when utility power is available and go into grid-tie mode to sell any incoming DC power beyond what's needed to trickle the batteries at a float charge. If the utility fails, they'll switch to battery power in about 20 milliseconds under most conditions. This is so fast you probably won't notice it happening. Outback inverters will accept generator input, and have robust built-in battery chargers, so these units could continue indefinitely without grid power, so long as you've got enough renewable energy input or generator fuel. Outback grid-tie Power Centers retail for around \$1.00 to \$1.40/watt; batteries not included. The larger dual-inverter units are more cost effective. Grid-tie Power Centers include the Mate, a remote monitor and control panel that also has an RS-232 output for computer monitoring.

Author Honesty, a Disclaimer: I've known and worked with Outback products and people for almost two decades. They're open, honest, and supportive, but haven't forgotten to have fun along the way. I like to see them succeed, because they build good equipment, and back it up with real expertise. I participated in beta testing of the MX60 charge control, and the grid-tie inverters; both outstanding pieces of hardware/software. Outback inverter serial numbers GFX0001 and GFX0002 live on my shop wall and have been doing flawless duty making my PG&E meter spin backwards most days.

◆ **Outback PS1 Power Center** The PS1 takes several standard Outback components and through tight design and clever packaging have managed to give us a 3,000 watt inverter/charger with an MPPT charge controller, a PV combiner, and all other necessary safety equipment as needed in a package only 17.25"wide x 31.3"high x 12.5"deep. A separate battery box of the same width is available that will take four 100 amp-hour sealed batteries. The complete pre-wired, UL-approved NEMA 3R assembly is everything you need for grid-tie with modest battery backup, and fits in a space 18" wide by 6 feet high. It comes equipped with lockable covers for indoor or outdoor installation. These are the same exact components, with the same performance, as used on the larger Power Centers described above, it's just packaged tighter, and there's no room for a second inverter later on if you decide to expand. The PS1 retails for about $1.40/watt; batteries not included.

SMA Sunny Island   *www.sma-america.com*

The Sunny Island is a unique battery-based 4,200-watt inverter package that can operate on- or off-grid. When the utility fails, the German-built Sunny Island uses stored battery energy to create an instant, stable, 120VAC signal within your home (or neighborhood, potentially), that allows any direct-tie inverters to keep operating. So rather than connecting your PV array to a charge controller for battery charging, the Sunny Island connects the PV to a direct grid-tie inverter like the Sunny Boy. If the utility power fails, the Sunny Island uses battery energy to create grid-like power that's obviously going to keep your appliances happy, and fools any direct-tie inverters into thinking the grid is still up. The direct-tie power will be used to run your house, and if there's still power available, recharge the Sunny Island's batteries. Once the batteries have recharged, if there's still excess power available (and the utility grid hasn't come back), the Sunny Island will shift the 60 hz frequency slightly to turn off the direct-tie inverter(s). If it's nighttime, or there's insufficient PV power being input, then stored battery power makes up the shortfall. If batteries get low, an on-board generator management system will automatically start your

Outback's PS1 Power Center (as seen with x-ray vision). *Photo courtesy of Outback Power Systems.*

backup generator. If the generator fails, or there isn't one, a load shedding relay can turn off selected non-critical loads when the batteries reach a slightly lower point.

The Sunny Island is particularly good if your PV array needs to be a long distance away, since all power transmission is at 120VAC or 240VAC. It can also be used to create a grid, where none exists, for several homes or outbuildings in a remote neighborhood. Multiple direct-tie inverters and multiple Sunny Islands can all be tied together in a large grid covering many square miles. This could be just the ticket for a big, spread out eco-resort.

The Sunny Island delivers 4,200 watts continuously, or two to three times that wattage for progressively shorter periods. Two units can be stacked for 240-volt output, and multiple single or stacked units can co-exist on a single grid system. Because the Sunny Island doesn't work directly with a PV array, it probably doesn't qualify for rebates in most states. (But the Sunny Boy connected to the PV array does qualify.)

Sunny Island inverter for on- and off-grid needs. *Photo courtesy of SMA-America.*

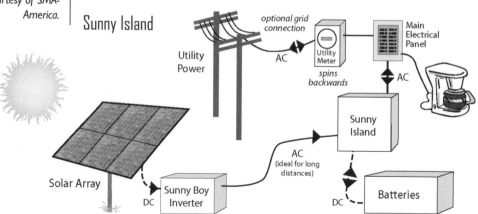

Sunny Island

Safety Equipment

Every renewable energy installation is going to have a few bits of system-specific safety equipment in the form of combiner boxes, disconnects, fuses, ground-fault protection, and a few other gizmos that quickly cause your eyes to glaze over, and start skipping ahead. Right. There's no sex appeal in safety, so we'll cover this quickly. Just remember...this stuff keeps your house from burning down! (Got your attention now?)

DC Combiner Boxes
PV modules are wired in "series-strings." A string might only be one module for a 12-volt battery system, or it could be up to 24 modules for some direct grid-tied inverters. Generally, if there's two or less series strings in a system, an unfused combiner box is used to wire the strings together. With three or more strings, a fused combiner is used, since if one string or module is shorted out, there's the potential for more amperage from the combined strings than the module wiring or J-box is rated to handle. Combiners may be roof, rack, or wall-mounted.

An Outback combiner box with a lightning arrestor on the left side. *Photo by Doug Pratt.*

DC Disconnect
Electrical code requires a manual disconnect between any power source and any appliance. This is so the appliance can be removed for service or repair without leaving hot wiring exposed. In our systems, power sources are the PV array, and possibly a wind turbine and battery bank. Appliances are the inverter and, in battery systems, the charge controller.

For lower voltage battery-based systems, the disconnect is simply a couple of $40 circuit breakers on either side of the charge controller, and a bigger more expensive circuit breaker between the battery and inverter.

For direct grid-tied systems we're usually working with much higher voltages, typically 250 to 550 volts, so more specialized equipment rated for up to 600 volts is called for. Aesthetic it isn't. Safe and necessary it is. The Square D brand HU361RB disconnect has a special UL listing for high voltage DC. It's that gray box with the handle on the side next to almost every grid-tied inverter picture we've shown you in this entire book. With single-channel inverters up to about 3,000 watts, a single HU361RB will service up to three inverters. The Sharp inverter has three-channels internally, so each SunVista inverter requires its own gray box.

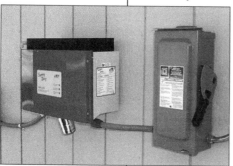

HU361RB disconnect (right) and a Sunny Boy inverter with small lightning arrestor on the bottom (left).

For inverters outputting 4,000 watts or more, we usually end up with three series PV strings or more, so fusing is required. The H361RB (a fused version of the Square D brand disconnect) is often used, since it includes combiner, fusing, and disconnect functions all in one box.

Lightning Protection

Some sort of lightning protection is a good idea on any of these systems. How seriously you consider lightning protection depends mostly on where you live. Californians can take a pretty relaxed attitude; Floridians need all the help they can muster.

Lightning wants to go to ground. Your job is to give it an easy, obvious path, and then stay out of the way. In all cases, lightning protection begins with grounding the nice electrically transmissive aluminum frames of your modules; not the mounting structure—you want to ground right to the module frame. This ground needs to connect to the main household ground rod. If there's a secondary ground rod at the array, that's fine, but all ground rods in the system need to connect together. Good grounding will divert better than 90 percent of strikes harmlessly. Beyond grounding there are inexpensive $50 absorbers (also called lighting arrestors; see above photo). Delta is the common brand; PolyPhaser offers better protection for those solar systems in serious need of lightning protection. Your installer should have a good idea how much of a threat lightning will be to your system. Check out this site to see a great map of lightning density in the U.S. www.lightningsafety.noaa.gov/lightning_map.htm

AC Disconnect

It isn't required by electrical code, or UL listings, but most utility companies require a lockable AC disconnect between their meter and your grid-tie device. This is so they can positively lock your grid-tie off if they're doing repairs in the area. It's a little baffling and frustrating as to why, since UL1741 (which every grid-tie inverter is certified to), has several layers of shut-off protection in case of utility failure. But it's their grid, and you've gotta play by their rules. For most residential systems this requirement will cost you under $100. If you have multiple inverters, you may have to install a small AC circuit breaker panel as an AC combiner box, since the AC disconnect is required to be a single lever.

The other sticking point here is that the disconnect usually has to be within 10 feet of the utility meter. Occasionally we've run into situations where the meter is down by the county road, while the house is several hundred yards up the hill. Rather than trench to the meter and run power down and back, the practical solution is to simply install a larger disconnect that will shut off the entire service to the house. The chance of the utility ever actually using the AC disconnect is infinitesimally small.

That concludes our safety section; back to our regular programming. Thank you for staying awake. You're officially safe now.

Wind Turbines

Big, heavy, and slow are what I like to see in a wind turbine. A big blade will catch more energy during the mild winds that most of the U.S. sees, thus producing more power every day. Since it's the single most important specification, we've listed the blade sweep area in square feet for each turbine. Nothing else will tell you as much about a turbine. Heavy construction means the machine won't be so

Blow Pollution Away

Over its approximate 20-year life, a small residential wind turbine can offset approximately 1.2 tons of air pollutants and 200 tons of greenhouse gases.

stressed during storms, and historically, the heavier the wind machine, the longer its life expectancy. Slow refers to the rotor speed. Slower machines are much quieter, bearings last longer, and there's less stress through the whole drivetrain. Now, the reality is that all these desirable features drive the price way up, so we need to reach a compromise between the ideal, and what's affordable. Let's look at what's typically available for residential use. (*Listed alphabetically*)

African Wind Power *www.abundantre.com*

I'll admit it upfront. This South African manufacturer comes closest to my ideal of big, heavy, and slow, while still remaining affordable.

African Wind Power 3.6 Model. *Photo courtesy of Abundant Renewable Energy.*

They currently offer the 3.6 model (that's the rotor diameter in meters) that has a sweep area of 109 square feet (10.1 square meters), which is huge for its rating of about 850 watts maximum when battery charging is at 24 volts; 1,000 watts at 48 volts; 1,600 watts for the direct grid-tie model. The tower top weight is 250 pounds, also huge for a turbine of this power. They've only been available in the U.S. for a couple years, and they've been upgrading bits and pieces as they've gone along, fine-tuning the design. Everyone who's flown one has good things to say about them, particularly that they're VERY quiet and dependable. The tower kits offered by the North American distributor are very complete with anchors and even a hoisting cable. AWP is rumored to be coming out with a larger 7.2 model in the near future. Retail prices are around $3,300 for the 24- or 48-volt battery charging models with control/rectifier and diversion load. The grid-tie model with Windy Boy 1,800-watt inverter and a control/rectifier with diversion load is around $6,800. Tilt-up pipe tower kits of 43- to 127-feet are available for $1,700 to $3,700.

Bergey Windpower *www.bergey.com*

Bergey has been building heavy, dependable wind turbines in Norman, Oklahoma since 1980. They pioneered the simple side-furling design that practically all turbines use for overspeed protection now.

Bergey offers their small XL.1 with a 52.8 square feet (4.9 square meters) sweep area and a maximum output of 1,000 watts in 24-volt DC trim only. (A 48-volt unit, and a direct grid-tie unit are under development.) This 75-pound turbine was engineered in Oklahoma, and is manufactured in China. It's a good unit, but don't expect a lot from the modest blade unless you've got average winds over 10 mph. The XL.1 retails for $2,150. The tower kits they're offering are some of the best in the business. Tilt-up guyed-tower kits from 30- to 104-feet are available for $790 to $1,850.

Bergey also has their larger Excel turbine with a 380-square foot (35.3 square meters) sweep area and a maximum output of 10,000 watts in the grid-tie model, or 7,500 watts in 48-volt DC *(shown on page 73)*. This turbine has been in production since 1983, with hundreds of units installed. Built in Oklahoma, it's heavy (about 1,000 pounds) and dependable. If you've got serious wind, this is a serious turbine with any bugs long since worked out. The Excel retails for $19,900 to $24,750 with controller or grid-tie inverter, depending on model. Guyed lattice tower kits are available from 60- to 120-feet for $6,200 to $9,200.

Proven Wind Turbines *www.provenenergy.com*

Proven turbines are built in Scotland, where they have an intimate familiarity with some of the world's most brutal wind conditions. For residential use, these are the toughest, most durable turbines money can buy. And yes, you're going to pay for that durability. Using all non-corrosive, marine quality parts, these turbines are the ultimate in big, heavy, and slow. Having no tail, these are all downwind machines, with the blades downwind of the tower. The

Proven WT2500 wind turbine. *Photo courtesy of Proven Energy.*

In 2004, wind turbines generated about 42 billion kilowatt-hours (143 trillion Btus) annually in the U.S., or about 1.3% of demand. The Department of Energy plans to increase this to 5% of demand by 2010, and is on track with this ambitious upgrade.

blades have a unique polypropylene hinge built into them that allows the blade to cone inward as wind speed increases. So the higher the wind speed, the smaller the swept area. This very clever control allows continued operation under the harshest conditions. There is no wind speed at which these turbines will stop producing, up to 145 mph!

Three models are offered by the U.S. distributor: 1) A 155-pound, 600-watt unit with a sweep area of 55.4 square feet (5.1 square meters) for battery charging; 2) A 418-pound, 2,500-watt unit with a swept area of 96.7 square feet (8.9 square meters) for battery charging or direct grid-tie with the Windy Boy 2500; and 3) An 1,100-pound, 6,000-watt model with 254 square feet (23.6 square meters) of sweep area for battery charging or direct grid-tie with a pair of Windy Boy 2500 inverters. Prices fluctuate with exchange rates. In early-2005 prices were about $5,500 for the 600-watt, $11,000 to $13,000 for the 2,500-watt, and $21,000 to $26,000 for the 6,000-watt. Proven has some aesthetically-gorgeous, self-supporting mono-pole towers, and conventional tilt-up guyed pipe towers.

Southwest Windpower Turbines www.windenergy.com

Southwest Windpower has been making small wind generators in northern Arizona since the late 1980s. They're the predominant residential-sized turbine manufacturer in North America with four primary models available. In the mid-90s Southwest introduced the swoopy all-cast-in-one-piece Air series of 300- and 400-watt turbines. These were so successful, and generated so much cash, that Southwest bought their chief competitor, World Power Technologies (who produced the Whisper 1000 turbines).

This is where our balance between the ideal big, heavy, and slow turbine has perhaps tipped too far toward the affordable. Whisper turbines tend to be small, lightweight, fast, and affordable, but strong or erratic winds over time may cause need for warranty repairs. If you have serious winds, you may want to consider other options.

◆ **Air-series** The cute little Air turbine has sold more units than any other wind generator. But with only 11.5 square feet (1.06 square meters) of sweep area, don't expect a lot of power from it. Current models are rated at 400 watts peak, although independent tests indicate it falls short of that. Good looks are the Air's strongest feature. Their powder-coated marine model is well-received, and you'll see them on sailboats worldwide. This is a high-speed turbine and it gets noisy at high wind speeds. The current model, the Air-X retails for $650 for the land version, or $875 for the powder-coated marine version, and weighs in at 13 pounds either way. Tilt-up guyed pipe tower kits of 25- or 47-feet are available for $190 or $260. You supply the 1.5-inch pipe.

◆ **Whisper 100** (*formerly the H40*) This turbine (*shown on page 69*) is quite specifically made for high-wind sites. It has a relatively small blade, 38.5 square feet (3.6 square meters) of sweep area, attached to a fairly large generator with 900 watts maximum. It weighs 47 pounds. If you don't have 12 mph or higher average winds, this isn't your turbine. The new 100 model has a long list of upgrades and improvements over the H40, so Southwest is responding positively to problems and low-life expectancy of the old H40. The new model also has a longer five-year warranty. Retail price of this turbine is about $1,900 including controller. Tilt-up guyed pipe tower kits are available from 24- to 80-feet at $300 to $950. You supply the 2.5-inch pipe.

◆ **Whisper 200** (*formerly the H80*) This turbine is a better choice for most folks with moderate winds. It has a relatively good-sized blade of 78.5 square-foot (7.3 square meters) sweep area on a modest 1,000-watt maximum generator, with a weight of 65 pounds. This turbine will perform well under the modest winds that most of North America sees most of the time. The new 200 model has a long list of

Southwest's Air series wind turbine. *Photo courtesy of Southwest Windpower.*

upgrades and improvements over the former H80, and has a longer five-year warranty. Retail price of this turbine is about $2,400 including controller. Tilt-up guyed pipe tower kits are the same as Whisper 100 model.

A new grid-tie version of the Whisper 200 with a Windy Boy 2500 inverter is available for $5,200. The same tower kits apply.

◆ **Whisper 500** (*formerly the 175*) Like other models in the Whisper line, this turbine with 172 square feet (16.0 square meters) of sweep area, has just received a complete overhaul and upgrade— and this was perhaps the model that needed it the most. The former 175 was a lightweight 3,000-watt turbine that didn't hold up well under stronger winds. The new model now has standard side-furling, and all the bits and pieces prone to early wear have been eliminated

Comparison of Popular Wind Turbines

	Proven Engineering WT600	SouthWest Windpower Whisper 100	Bergey Windpower XL.1	SouthWest Windpower Whisper 200	African Wind Power 3.6	Proven Engineering WT2500	Bergey Excel
Rated Power	600 watts	900 watts	1.0 kW	1.0 kW	1.0 kW (DC) 1.6 kW (AC)	2.5 kW	7.5 kW (DC) 10 kW (AC)
Cut-in wind speed	6.0 mph	7.5 mph	5.6 mph	7.0 mph	6.0 mph	6.0 mph	7.0 mph
Rated wind speed	26 mph	28 mph	24.6 mph	26 mph	25 mph	26 mph	31 mph
RPM @ rated output	500 rpm	1,500 rpm	490 rpm	900 rpm	350 rpm	300 rpm	300 rpm
Approximate monthly kWhs @ 12 mph	124 kWh	105 kWh	188 kWh	193 kWh	192 kWh	415 kWh	900 kWh (DC) 1,090 kWh (AC)
Rotor Diameter	8.4 feet	7.0 feet	8.2 feet	10.0 feet	11.8 feet	11.1 feet	23.0 feet
Maximum design wind speed	145 mph	120 mph	120 mph	120 mph	>100 mph	145 mph	120 mph
Turbine Weight	154 lb.	47 lb.	75 lb.	65 lb.	250 lb.	418 lb.	1000 lb.
Direct Grid-Tie	no	no	no	yes	yes	yes	yes

SOURCES: Bergey Windpower, Southwest Windpower, Solar Wind Works, Abundant Renewable Energy, *Home Power* Magazine

or upgraded, so it deserves a fresh evaluation that only time will provide. This is the last of the two-bladed turbines, which are easier and cheaper to manufacture, but don't deal with shifting winds very well at all. If your winds blow steadily from one direction, two-blade turbines are great. When winds are shifting they suffer a lot of heavy vibration. The 500 model retails for $7,095 including controller. It weighs about 155 pounds. Tilt-up guyed pipe tower kits are available from 30- to 70-feet at $980 to $1,455. This turbine wants 5-inch pipe for its tower, which is sometimes a difficult size to find. Tower kits supply the hardware and cabling, you supply the pipe.

System Monitors

Good digital monitoring mounted on or in the inverter has pretty much become the industry standard. There are some models that still call it an option and charge a bit extra, but they're the exception. However, monitoring at the inverter requires you walk out to wherever the inverter is. Want it more convenient? The next level is to get the information inside your house, or better yet, inside your computer, and maybe to save some bits of it every day. If this is your goal, shop carefully, as some inverter manufacturers make this as easy as plugging in a couple Ethernet cables, others require the addition of some slightly pricy options, and a few just don't make it possible at all. Details vary with every manufacturer. There are also after-market manufacturers who make software solutions for remote monitoring or even web-based monitoring beyond what the original equipment makers can provide. Check out Fat Spaniel (*www.fatspaniel.com*) and Right Hand Engineering (*www.righthandeng.com*).

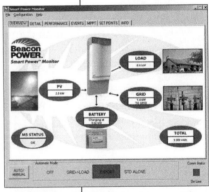

Beacon offers a very complete monitoring and control package for PC-based computers.

Outback's MX60 controller with MPPT controls. *Photo courtesy of Outback Power Systems.*

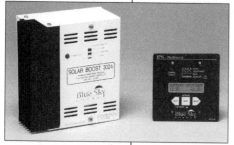

Blue Sky's 3024i charge controller and monitor. *Photo courtesy of Blue Sky.*

Charge Controllers (battery-based systems only)

Until a few years ago, the charge controller's job in a battery-based grid-tie system was pretty minimal. It was only there in case the utility failed on a sunny day, and the house wasn't using all the available incoming power. Only then did it get to be anything more than a simple connection that turned on at dawn and off at dusk. All the rest of the time the inverter monitored the battery voltage, and sucked off any power beyond what was needed to maintain a gentle float voltage. Then Maximum Power Point Tracking for charge controllers was developed. By running the PV array at whatever voltage delivers the greatest wattage, and then downconverting that higher voltage into amps the battery can digest, our PV array can average about 15 percent more energy output over the year.

Given the large size of most grid-tied systems, the addition of an MPPT charge controller is like having an extra two or three modules in the system. This is an expense that more than pays for itself immediately. There are currently two manufacturers offering large MPPT controls: Outback has their masterful MX60 controller, and Blue Sky (formerly RV Power Products) has their line of 30-, 50-, and 60-amp controls. Blue Sky Energy was the first out of the box and their units are better than average, but Outback's MX60 is more efficient and adaptable. The MX60 allows charging any battery voltage between 12 and 60 volts, with any array voltage that's under 150 volts open circuit. (Array voltage must be higher than battery voltage.) Since higher voltage transmits easier, this means smaller wire sizes and less transmission loss.

Xantrex has been rumoring they would come out with an MPPT-based line of charge controllers, but as of spring 2005, we haven't seen them yet.

MPPT Technology: Squeezing the Last Watt from Your Array

Solar modules are designed to operate at higher voltages than they are nominally rated for. There are two main reasons for this. Since voltage always flows from a higher potential to a lower one, the modules in battery-based systems need to operate at a high enough voltage to charge the batteries in both low light conditions (when the array voltage drops), and when the batteries reach a high state of charge. Since lead-acid batteries (in a nominal 12-volt system) often reach potentials as high as 15.5 volts during equalization, the array's rated voltage must be even higher. Typically, this will be in the range of 16.5 to 18 volts. During the bulk charging stage, a typical charge controller will simply hook the array directly to the batteries. The batteries, of course, don't have any use for all that extra voltage, so they pull the array voltage down to a comfortable level.

Let's take a typical 120-watt module rated for 7.10 amps at 16.9 volts (7.10 x 16.9 = 119.99). How does this play out in the real world? Well, when your batteries are at 12.5 volts and they're drawing all 7.10 amps, the module is only producing 88.75 watts, or about 74 percent of its rated output. As the batteries reach a higher state of charge the percentage will go up, but there is always a significant percentage of power that is lost.

MPPT (Maximum Power Point Tracking) charge controllers get around this problem by using a high-frequency DC to DC converter to provide a voltage the batteries are happy with.

In the process, it uses the extra voltage to produce usable amperage in excess of what the modules were designed to produce. The trick is, the modules don't know this. They just think the batteries are finally getting their act together.

In battery-based systems, power point tracking works best when there is a large disparity between the module voltage and the battery voltage. This most often occurs when the batteries are partly discharged, under a considerable load, or when the modules are cold. As the batteries reach a higher state of charge, loads are decreased, or sunlight heats up the modules, the extra power gained from MPPT diminishes.

Direct grid-tied inverters also use MPPT technology to level out the voltage changes brought on by time-of-day and weather-related changes, thus providing the inverter with a consistent voltage input. Just like in a battery-based system, MPPT squeezes the last available watt out of the array, while maximizing inverter efficiency at the same time.

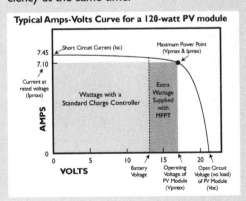

Typical Amps-Volts Curve for a 120-watt PV module

What's a SMALL Battery?

In the context we're talking here – battery banks that can run a house for hours – a **small** battery is anything near the size you might find under the hood of a car. In battery nomenclature, these would be group 24, 27, or 31 batteries with up to about 100 amp-hours capacity, and weighing as much as 75 pounds. **Medium**-size batteries go from 100 amp-hours up to around 400. Anything with 500 or more amp-hours is officially **big**.

Batteries

We've said it throughout this book, and we'll keep saying it: if you're using batteries for emergency backup duty, use sealed batteries! Although they're more expensive initially, you'll get better life expectancy, and better performance out of them, compared to conventional wet-cell batteries (the kind you take the caps off to add water). There are two types of sealed lead-acid batteries, with slight construction differences. AGM and gel are the two contenders for your dollar.

AGM (Absorbed Glass Mat) **batteries** have lead plates wrapped in a fiberglass type material that holds a minimum of liquid electrolyte. AGM cells are less fussy to build, and usually cost less than true gel batteries. Because the electrolyte is liquid and can move around a bit, they tend to tolerate high charge and discharge rates quite well. What they won't tolerate is high voltage. The charging voltage must never be allowed above 2.35 volts per cell. Higher voltages cause gassing, which vents water vapor...which AGM batteries can't afford to lose, and have no mechanism to replace. Even a single overcharge will damage AGM cells.

Gel batteries have the electrolyte in a jellied form. They're more difficult to build because no air voids can be allowed when filling the battery with gel. Voids won't simply bubble up and dissipate—they create a dead space on the plate forever. Gel batteries start their life with more moisture, so they're more tolerant of the occasional overcharge. Still, 2.35 volts per cell is usually the recommended maximum charge voltage. Although they're more expensive initially, gel cells usually deliver slightly better life expectancy than AGM cells.

In all cases, bigger batteries last longer. Your battery bank will need a certain amp-hours capacity in order to deliver the backup power you need. You could build that bank out of many smaller batteries, or a few larger batteries. The bank with a few large batteries will last longer, be less prone to charging and performance problems, and cost you less per year. Count on it!

There are several sealed battery distributors we can recommend based on good experiences, or your dealer may have a good source already. If not, check these:

MK Batteries *www.mkbattery.com*
These folks distribute Deka brand batteries, which are well-regarded in NREL testing. They offer both AGM and true gel batteries in small to medium, or 50 to 225 amp-hour sizes through a widely scattered network of warehouses that'll save you cross-country shipping costs.

MK's 8G31 12-volt sealed gel-type battery is a tried-and-true favorite. *Photo courtesy of MK Batteries.*

Concorde Batteries *www.concordebattery.com*
Their Sun Xtender line is an AGM product designed specifically for the solar industry. They have a strong dependable track record and a number of dealers who feel their batteries deliver the best service for the money. They offer small to large sizes of 50 to 600 amp-hours. *(See photo on page 49.)*

Hawker Batteries *www.hawkerpowersource.com*
The Envirolink line are the largest gel batteries, with the longest life expectancy available. These large cells are often used for electric forklift service, and will typically see a 15- to 20-year life expectancy doing "easy" emergency backup service. These are shipped in steel packs of six or twelve cells, and will require a forklift to unload. They're available in sizes from 370 to 1,480 amp-hours. ❖

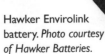

Hawker Envirolink battery. *Photo courtesy of Hawker Batteries.*

Got Lightning? Go Solar

Neither rain, nor lightning, nor hurricane-force winds shall stay this faithful accountant from the swift completion of his appointed duties. No, John Kerr never actually said that, but it seems to be the Florida tax accountant's operating principle, nonetheless. Not only did his home survive direct hits from Hurricanes Jeanne and Frances in the fall of 2004, his home office never lost power, even though the grid was down for days at a time following each storm.

It wasn't hurricanes, however, as much as the frequent, grid-busting lightning storms around Port St. Lucie that provided the original prodding for John to install his simple-yet-functional 12-volt PV system. Consisting of six 90-watt roof-mounted Matrix modules, a quartet of Best Power 12-volt, 135-amp hour sealed UPS batteries, and a 1,500-watt Coleman Powermate modified-sinewave

inverter, this small but adequate system powers John's accounting office and the home's security system, as well as the garage and all of the power tools John uses when he's not chasing down loopholes in the tax code. A separate 24-volt system runs the pumps that circulate hot water from the single roof-mounted solar hot-water panel. And, to keep watt-gobbling artificial lighting to a minimum, a trio of tube skylights brings an abundance of natural light into the office, and the home he shares with his wife Kathleen, and son, Ian.

The system is not configured to allow John's homegrown wattage to pass from his array into the Florida Power & Light grid, nor could it be, without an approved inverter. But that doesn't prevent John from drawing power from the grid—with the aid of a manual bypass switch—on those rare occasions when he needs a little extra power.

All told, it's a clever, inexpensive solution to a persistent problem. But, hey—isn't that what we expect from our tax accountants?

Top closeup photo shows the PV panels on Kerr's roof. *Photos by John Kerr.*

CHAPTER TWELVE

Who Does The Installation?

D o we have you thinking more seriously about an alternative energy
system yet? Good. This is something that's going to return security and comfort for many years to come. Now comes the decision of
whether to hire a contractor, or do some or all of the installation
yourself.

Finding and Qualifying a Contractor

If you live in a state like California or New Jersey that has an active,
well-funded rebate program, then finding a contractor is easy...maybe
too easy. Don't be fooled by companies that have a lot of money
to spend on newspaper ads and slick literature. Often the low-
profile installer with low overhead can do the job more to your
satisfaction, so get more than one quote and study each quote
carefully. One advantage of doing a lot of solar installs, of course,
is that crews not only get faster, they get better. (Oh gee, we
won't make *that* mistake again!) Look in your Yellow Pages
under "SOLAR." You can also call your state energy office for
referrals *(see listings in appendix)*. Another source of quality
installers is the North American Board of Certified Energy
Practitioners (NABCEP). It's a mouthful, but it is the only

20,000 and Counting!

Over 20,000 grid-tied
homes in the United
States now utilize
photovoltaics.

Source: SolarBuzz.com

organization currently testing and certifying solar electric installers. This is a voluntary program and is not inexpensive or easy. So these are folks who are serious about being professional and knowledgeable. Find them, and a list of certified installers, sorted by state at: *www.nabcep.org.*

In order to give a realistic quote, a contractor absolutely needs to perform a site inspection. All houses are different, with roofs that face in every direction, covered with a variety of materials, and shaded by who knows what. If a contractor is willing to give a firm quote without at least a drive-by, you should be very suspicious. If you have any trees, buildings, dormers, or other potential obstructions you should absolutely expect someone to show up with a ladder and a Solar Pathfinder device that will show what's going to create shading problems, and when. (Obviously the ladder is only needed with roof-mounted arrays.) The Solar Pathfinder shows the solar window where it is right now, so you need to get the Pathfinder to where the array is potentially going to be.

The Solar Pathfinder is a clever device that instantly shows what time of day and months of the year shading will be a problem for your solar array.

Payment schemes vary. Because the state agencies that approve rebates are often backlogged weeks or even months, expecting full payment at the beginning of the process isn't realistic. Someone other than you gets to sit on your cash all that time. You should expect to put down a substantial down payment of $1,000 to $5,000 and sign a contract, with the balance due on completion of the installation. If you find a contractor who's willing to accept the state rebate in lieu of payment from you, that's a real plus. Those are dollars that never need to leave your pocket. And since the contractor can't claim the rebate until the job is signed off by the local electrical inspector, you're assured a speedy, proper installation.

And finally, make sure your contractor is licensed. All but a couple very rural states require electrical workers to be licensed. You can usually find their state license number imprinted on their business card, stationary, and email. Most state contractor licensing boards have convenient websites where you can quickly check to see if a contractor's license is valid, current, and if there are any pending complaints or actions. For a website with links to all state contractor licensing boards, visit the Contractor's License Reference Site at: *www.contractors-license.org*.

Do the Installation Yourself?

Unless you've done this before, we're going to suggest that installing a grid-tie system isn't a good project to undertake entirely by yourself. Because of the slow, complex, and sometimes baffling paperwork required, and because it requires working with lethally-high voltages, we recommend that your best option for cutting the cost is to hire a pro, and become his or her helper. And even if you are a pro already, many programs have a self-install penalty. In California and New Jersey for instance, there's a 15 percent reduction in rebate for self-installing. So it's best to hire a contractor. With the extra 15 percent rebate you can afford it.

You can still shop for, and buy, all the major components yourself, saving the contractor mark-up on parts. There are a number of retailers willing to sell directly to end users, with varying levels of customer support. Some offer very complete standardized packages, while others will customize a package to suit your available space and budget. But watch out! If you web browse for the absolutely lowest price, you can expect absolutely no service or support to go with it. You'd best know what you're doing. Also, watch out for long delivery times. The real lowball dealers won't even order your hardware until they get your check. (How do you suppose they pay for it?) With modules in short supply and everybody on an allocation waiting list, this sets you up for a several-month wait with your money already

Hands-On Guide
If you feel this is something you can tackle successfully, here's some more info and guidance to help you along. *A Guide to Photovoltaic (PV) System Design and Installation* by Bill Brooks of Endecon Engineering can't be beat. Through his amazing classes Bill has educated hundreds of professional California solar installers. Here it is distilled for the taking: *www.energy.ca.gov/reports/ 2001-09-04_500-01-020.PDF.*

gone. Ideally, you will want a retailer who's supplying a schematic drawing of your system (see examples below), offers technical support by phone and/or email, and can deliver your hardware within 3 – 4 weeks. The schematic drawing is particularly important. Not only is this your installation road map showing how everything connects together, and with what gauge wire, but most building departments now require one before they'll issue a permit. (And you've **got** to get a permit if you want a rebate!) If your dealer doesn't supply a schematic, guess who's going to? ❖

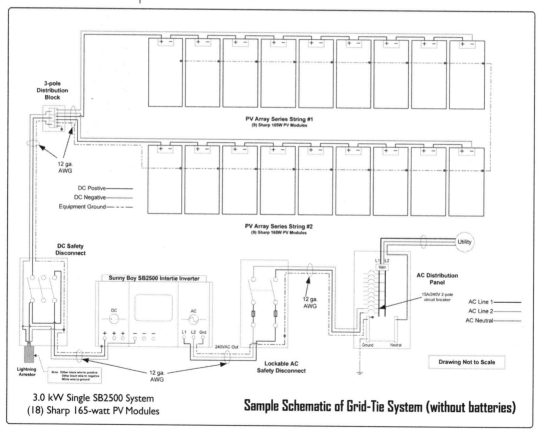

3.0 kW Single SB2500 System
(18) Sharp 165-watt PV Modules

Sample Schematic of Grid-Tie System (without batteries)

Our two sample schematics are both using 18 Sharp 165-watt solar modules. Notice how much more complex the battery-based system is. This is why battery systems cost more. In addition to the batteries, there's more safety and control equipment required. *Schematics by Doug Pratt.*

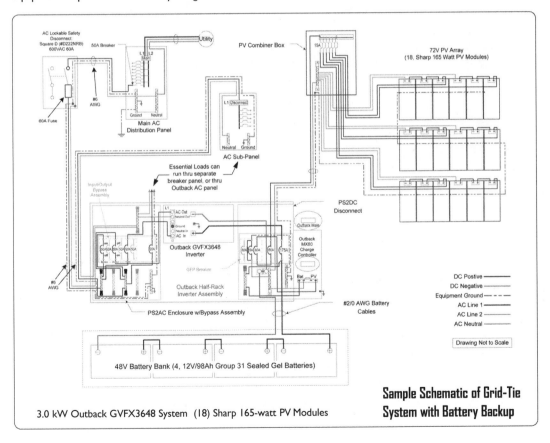

3.0 kW Outback GVFX3648 System (18) Sharp 165-watt PV Modules

Sample Schematic of Grid-Tie System with Battery Backup

A typical rooftop installation in Healdsburg, California with UniRac rails on standoffs supporting 20 Astropower (now G.E.) 120-watt modules. Standoffs are optional on conventional asphalt shingle roofs like this, but are higher-quality and less likely to leak. Excess rail length was trimmed after all the modules were secured.

The Sunny Boy 2500 is mounted on a north-facing outside wall, with the standard Square D brand DC disconnect on the near side, and the AC disconnect on the far side. Wiring from the AC disconnect to the adjacent circuit breaker panel runs inside the wall. This would be a typical one-day installation for an experienced crew of two or three.

Photos courtesy of Summit Electrical Service, Santa Rosa, California.

Postscript

In 1966, in a little-known book titled *Building Blocks of the Universe* Isaac Asimov wrote, with customary prescience, "Recently, solar batteries have been designed which can produce an electric current when exposed to sunlight. So far, such batteries are only laboratory curiosities, but the day may come when they will be an important source of power for mankind."

An insightful call from a great science writer. But not even a visionary like Asimov could have guessed back then the extent to which the science and applicability of solar "batteries"—as solar cells were originally called—could have advanced in the course of a few decades. From laboratory curiosity, to the space program and a few limited terrestrial applications, and finally to the ubiquitous solar arrays powering millions of homes and villages worldwide, solar electricity has at last come of age.

But, as widespread and accessible as the technology may be today, what we see around us is merely the beginning. If we're lucky, forty years down the road solar technologies—and their sidekick, wind—will have made great strides toward replacing coal-fired and nuclear power plants. Cars that once ran on gasoline will run on hydrogen cleaved from water or biomass by solar and wind applications. Homes will be routinely designed to make the most of their natural settings for lighting, heating and cooling, and all the extra energy needed to power them and keep us in the comfort zone will be derived from environmentally-responsible sources.

In time, the absurdity of the self-destructive conventions we cling to in the name of progress will become universally evident. Future generations will look back on our current energy production practices

Photo by LaVonne Ewing

with a mixture of bemusement and revulsion, much as we now look back at the barbaric and superstitious medical procedures of the Middle Ages.

Until then, we can each help to ensure a long, bright future for a really spectacular planet by spurning the unchecked burning of fossil fuels, one solar or wind application at a time.

So, what are you waiting for?

Got Sun? Go Solar!

Acknowledgments

Any book, even one as seemingly simple as this one, is the work of far more people than the authors. Sure, we write all the words and get our names on the cover in big letters, but without the assistance of scads of others who toiled in the background to turn a raw manuscript into a bona fide book with lots of pictures and stories, the result wouldn't be anything you'd want to read. So it's only fair we take the time to thank everyone who went out of their way to make us look good.

First and foremost, we'd like to thank LaVonne Ewing, who humbled us both by working harder and complaining less than either of us glory hogs. Without her organizational skills and design talents *Got Sun? Go Solar* would never have sprouted wings. As an editor, she can nurse a crippled phrase to a perfect state of health, or axe a misbegotten one so painlessly it seems an act of mercy. Thanks, LaVonne—you're the best.

We'd also like to thank all the homeowners who provided photographs of their grid-tied homes, and happily agreed to being a part of this book. You are an inspiration to us all.

Home-based solar and wind energy systems would still occupy the realm of science fiction without the hundreds of companies and corporations who believed so strongly in the concept of renewable energy that they were willing to risk it all by engineering and manufacturing the state-of-the-art components needed to harness the power of the sun and wind. Many of them provided photographs and much of the hard-to-find information that helped to make this book what it is. We thank you, one and all.

And finally, we'd like to thank the diligent women and men at the National Renewable Energy Laboratory. You saw the grail when it was invisible to the rest of us, and broke the trail we all continue to follow. Without you, this would be a really short and boring book.

Tips on Appliances and Energy Conservation

Use compact fluorescent light bulbs...they add up to big energy savings. For example: if 6 bulbs are on for 5 hours a day: 60-watt incandescent bulbs will use 1,800 watt hours per day; 13-watt compact fluorescent bulbs will use only 390 watt hours.

Low-usage, high energy appliances (hair dryers, microwaves, coffer makers, etc.) are not much of a problem since they draw very little power when averaged out over time. You can also choose not to use them, if you're low on power.

Invest in a new **refrigerator and/or freezer**. You'll be amazed at how much more energy-efficient they are. The typical new fridge now uses 80 percent less energy than models from the late 1980s and early 1990s. Do your research on *www.energystar.gov* before buying and always read those yellow tags!

If you want to cook when the grid is down, and you don't have battery backup, buy an **oven** with spark ignition instead of the typical glow bar. Glow bars use 300-400 watts ALL the time your oven is on. Peerless-Premier is one brand that is ideal for off-grid homes.

To conserve energy and water when washing clothes, a **front-loading clothes washer** is a must, as is a gas-fired clothes dryer. Better yet, use a clothesline or indoor rack for drying.

Instant water heaters, either gas or electric models, use 20 to 40 percent less energy because they only work when someone turns on the hot water faucet. They also last 30 – 40 years, reducing landfill and resource waste.

A **solar hot water** system uses NO energy (that you'll ever get a bill for). Combined with an instant water heater you've got the lowest-cost, and most ecologically-responsible way to heat domestic hot water.

One watt delivered for one hour = **one watt-hour** | 1,000 watt-hours = one **kWh**
amps x volts = watts (*2 amps x 120 volts = 240 watts*)

Energy Consumption of Appliances

Using a WATTS-UP? Meter, we measured the following appliances

Appliance	Continuous Draw (Watts)
Computer, desktop	90
Computer, laptop	24
17" monitor	100
17" LCD (flat screen) monitor	50
HP LaserJet printer (in use)	600
HP Inkjet printer (in use)	15
Microwave (full power)	1,400
Coffee Maker	900
Toaster, 2-slice	750
Amana Range (propane): Burners	0
Oven (with glow bar; when heating)	380
Electric Range (small/large burner)	1,250/2,100
Blender	350
Mixer	120
Slow Cooker (high/low)	240/180
20" Television	50
27" Television	120
50" LCD Television	175
Stereo System	25
Stereo, small portable	10
Vacuum, Oreck	410
Vacuum, Dirt Devil Upright	980
Table-top Fountain	5

Appliance	Continuous Draw (Watts)
Sewing Machine (Bernina)	70
Serger (Pfaff)	140
Clothes Dryer (propane)	300
Clothes Iron	1200
Hair Curling Iron	55
Hair Dryer (high/low)	1,500/400
Furnace Fan ($1/3$ hp / $1/2$ hp)	700/875
Guitar Amp (ave. volume)	45
Jimi Hendrix volume	8,500

Appliance	Watt Hours
Dishwasher, cool dry	736 watt-hours/load
Clothes Washer (front-loading)	145 watt-hours/load
Air Conditioning	1,500 watts/ton (or 10,000 Btu) of capacity

We have not listed refrigerators or freezers since their efficiency is getting better every year. Look at the **EnergyStar.gov** website for the latest ratings. There are many models at, or under, 400 kWh per year, or about 1 kWh per day.

U.S. Annual Wind Average

To view this map and individual states in color:
http://rredc.nrel.gov/wind/pubs/atlas/maps.html

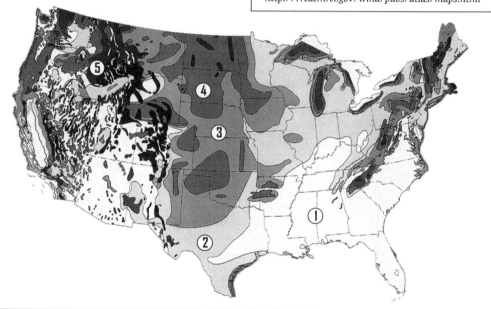

Wind Power Class	10 m (33 ft) tower		50 m (164 ft) tower	
	Wind Power W/m²	Speed m/s (mph)	Wind Power W/m²	Speed m/s (mph)
1	0	0	0	0
	100	4.4 (9.8 mph)	200	5.6 (12.5 mph)
2	150	5.1 (11.5 mph)	300	6.4 (14.3 mph)
3	200	5.6 (12.5 mph)	400	7.0 (15.7 mph)
4	250	6.0 (13.4 mph)	500	7.5 (16.8 mph)
5	300	6.4 (14.3 mph)	600	8.0 (17.9 mph)
6	400	7.0 (15.7 mph)	800	8.8 (19.7 mph)
7	1000	9.4 (21.1 mph)	2000	11.9 (26.6 mph)

System Sizing Worksheet — Your Electrical Needs

Electrical Device	Wattage (volts x amps)	X	Hours of Daily Use	x	Days Used per Week	÷	7	=	Ave. Daily Watt-Hours
		X		X		÷	7		
		X		X		÷	7		
		X		X		÷	7		
		X		X		÷	7		
		X		X		÷	7		
		X		X		÷	7		
		X		X		÷	7		
		X		X		÷	7		
		X		X		÷	7		
		X		X		÷	7		
		X		X		÷	7		
		X		X		÷	7		
		X		X		÷	7		
		X		X		÷	7		
		X		X		÷	7		

*15% to 25% is added to compensate for inefficiencies in the system (batteries, inverter, line loss)

Total Average Watt-Hours per Day

15% Loss Correction Factor*   x 1.15

Adjusted Average Watt-Hours per Day

Solar Insolation Data
Maps for Winter and Summer

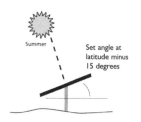

Set angle at latitude minus 15 degrees

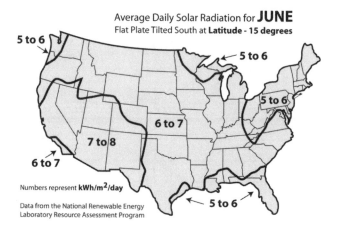

Average Daily Solar Radiation for **JUNE**
Flat Plate Tilted South at **Latitude - 15 degrees**

5 to 6

5 to 6

5 to 6

6 to 7

7 to 8

6 to 7

5 to 6

Numbers represent **kWh/m^2/day**

Data from the National Renewable Energy Laboratory Resource Assessment Program

---

U.S. Solar Radiation Resource Maps
http://rredc.nrel.gov/solar/old_data/nsrdb/redbook/atlas

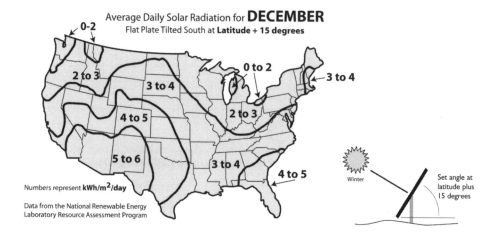

Average Daily Solar Radiation for **DECEMBER**
Flat Plate Tilted South at **Latitude + 15 degrees**

0-2

2 to 3

3 to 4

0 to 2

3 to 4

4 to 5

2 to 3

5 to 6

3 to 4

4 to 5

Numbers represent **kWh/m^2/day**

Data from the National Renewable Energy Laboratory Resource Assessment Program

Set angle at latitude plus 15 degrees

Solar Array Sizing Worksheet

	June	*Example*	December
1. Input your **Adjusted Ave. Watt-Hours per Day** from page 135.	_____	3000	_____
2. Find your site on the maps on the opposite page and input the nearest figure.	_____	6	_____
3. To find the number of watts you need to generate per hour of full sun, divide line 1 by line 2.	_____	500	_____
4. Select a solar module and multiply its rated wattage by .70 (.80 if using an MPPT charge controller). *Example: Enter 84 for a 120-watt module(or 96 with MPPT).* *	_____	84	_____
5. To find the number of modules needed, divide line 3 by line 4. **	_____	*6*	_____

* You'll only get 120 watts from a 120-watt PV module when using an MPPT charge controller during the 2 hours nearest high noon, and **only** when the surface temperature of the module is below 77 degrees Fahrenheit...which is hardly ever. Output is typically derated to 60% - 70% for standard charge controllers (75% - 80% with MPPT) to give you a more accurate number.

** The exact number of modules you need will be determined by the system voltage, since modules are wired together in series strings to achieve a voltage within the range required by the charge controller or inverter.

Electrical Formulas and Helpful Information

Calculating Line Loss

For a long time, I have wanted to know what the exact voltage drop would be in the wires if I added two modules to the solar array. By looking at standard wire loss tables I could see that it would be more than 2 percent, and less than 5 percent, but that wasn't close enough. Finally, I found the formula in *Pocket Ref*, a tight little book with more tables and formulas than I ever knew existed.

Following is an abbreviated version. It will work for all DC wiring, and all single-phase AC wiring, using copper wire below 121 degrees Fahrenheit. (For 3-phase AC, or aluminum wire, the complete formula can be found in the *Pocket Ref* by Thomas J. Glover, Sequoia Publishing Inc.)

EXAMPLE:
You want to run 70 feet of #2 wire for a 1,000-watt array, operating at 24 volts. What is the exact voltage drop?

First calculate the amps by dividing the watts (1,000) by the volts (24) = 41.66 amps. Then find the Wire Area in the chart on the next page for #2 wire (66,400). Plug the numbers into the formula:

Voltage Drop = $\dfrac{22 \times 70 \text{ feet} \times 41.66 \text{ amps}}{66,400}$

The voltage drop is .966 volts. To find the percentage of loss, divide .966 volts by your system voltage (24 volts) = .040, or 4% loss. *This amperage is possible only if the array is at peak output and you're using an MPPT charge controller. Normal output would be the module's rated amps (Ipmax).*

If you used #1 wire instead, the calculations would show a 3.1% loss; 1/0 wire will bring the voltage loss down to 2.5% ... a more acceptable number.

Using the Wire Size/Line Loss Tables

EXAMPLE:

Your 1,100 watt solar array is located 50 feet from the batteries. By referring to the Wire Size/Line Loss tables on the following pages, what size of wire do you need for a 2% loss?

48-volt System   #6 wire
24-volt System   1/0 wire *(over 4 times thicker wire than #6; and proportionately more expensive)*

EXAMPLE:

You have a well pump that draws 10 amps at 24-volts DC, and is 90 feet from the batteries. What size of wire do you need for a 2% loss?

By referring to the 24-Volt chart with 2% voltage drop, 10 amps going 90 feet would require #4 wire. If you settle for a 4% loss, you could use #6 wire, but the efficiency and life of the pump will be decreased.

Pocket Ref *states that "Voltage drop should be less than 2% if possible. If the drop is greater than 2%, efficiency of the equipment in the circuit is severely decreased and life of the equipment will be decreased. As an example, if the voltage drop on an incandescent light bulb is 10%, the light output of the bulb decreases over 30%!"*

1,000 watts = one **kilowatt** (kW)
1,000 kilowatts = one **megawatt** (MW)
1,000 megawatts = one **gigawatt** (GW)

Power Formula

watts = volts x amps

amps = watts / volts

Wire Area in Circular mils

4/0	212,000
3/0	168,000
2/0	133,000
1/0	106,000
#1	83,700
#2	66,400
#3	52,600
#4	41,700
#5	33,100
#6	26,300

$$\text{Actual Voltage Drop} = \frac{22 \times \text{length of wire in feet} \times \text{amps}}{\text{wire area in circular mils}}$$

Wire Size / Line Loss Tables

24 Volts DC : 2% Voltage Drop

Amps in Wire	Wattage at 24V	ONE-WAY DISTANCE FOR VARIOUS WIRE SIZES									
		#14	#12	#10	#8	#6	#4	#2	1/0	2/0	3/0
1	24	90	140	230	360	580	912	-	-	-	-
5	120	19	35	47	75	120	190	360	482	605	764
10	240	9	14	23	36	57	91	145	230	290	366
15	360	6	9	14	24	38	60	96	153	192	244
20	480	*	7	11	18	29	45	72	115	145	183
25	600	*	*	9	14	23	36	58	92	116	146
30	720	*	*	7	12	19	30	48	77	97	122
40	960	*	*	*	9	14	23	36	58	72	91
50	1200	*	*	*	*	11	18	29	46	58	73

48 Volts DC : 2% Voltage Drop

Amps in Wire	Wattage at 48V	ONE-WAY DISTANCE FOR VARIOUS WIRE SIZES									
		#14	#12	#10	#8	#6	#4	#2	1/0	2/0	3/0
1	48	180	280	460	720	-	-	-	-	-	-
5	240	39	62	99	157	250	397	632	-	-	-
10	480	18	28	46	72	114	182	290	460	580	732
15	720	12	18	28	48	76	120	192	306	384	488
20	960	*	14	22	36	58	90	144	230	290	366
25	1200	*	*	18	28	46	72	116	184	232	292
30	1440	*	*	14	24	38	60	96	154	194	244
40	1920	*	*	*	18	28	46	72	116	144	182
50	2400	*	*	*	*	22	36	58	92	116	146

*   Exceeds ampacity; do not use wire sizes in this zone; it may cause overheating.
-     Over 1,000 feet

One-way distances listed: measured from point A (such as the solar array) to point B (the batteries).
The **VOLTAGE DROP** refers to the percent of voltage lost due to resistance.
All distances calculated in feet for copper wire.

Wire Size / Line Loss Tables

120 Volts AC : 2% Voltage Drop

Amps in Wire	Wattage at 120VAC	ONE-WAY DISTANCE FOR VARIOUS WIRE SIZES									
		#14	#12	#10	#8	#6	#4	#2	1/0	2/0	3/0
1	120	450	710	1100	-	-	-	-	-	-	-
5	600	90	140	230	360	570	910	-	-	-	-
10	1200	45	71	110	180	290	460	720	-	-	-
15	1800	30	47	75	120	190	300	480	770	970	-
20	2400	*	36	57	90	140	230	360	580	730	920
25	3000	*	*	45	72	110	180	290	460	580	730
30	3600	*	*	38	60	95	150	240	380	480	610
40	4800	*	*	*	45	72	110	180	290	360	460
50	6000	*	*	*	*	57	91	140	230	290	370

240 Volts AC : 2% Voltage Drop

Amps in Wire	Wattage at 240VAC	ONE-WAY DISTANCE FOR VARIOUS WIRE SIZES									
		#14	#12	#10	#8	#6	#4	#2	1/0	2/0	3/0
1	240	900	-	-		-	-	-	-	-	-
5	1200	180	280	450	720	1100	-	-	-	-	-
10	2400	90	140	230	360	570	910	-	-	-	-
15	3600	60	95	150	240	380	610	970	-	-	-
20	4800	*	71	110	180	290	460	720	-	-	-
25	6000	*	*	91	140	230	360	580	920	-	-
30	7200	*	*	75	120	190	300	480	770	970	-
40	9600	*	*	*	90	140	230	360	580	730	920
50	12,000	*	*	*	*	110	180	290	460	580	730

*   Exceeds ampacity; do not use wire sizes in this zone; it may cause overheating.
-     Over 1,000 feet

One-way distances listed: measured from point A (such as the inverter) to point B (the AC house panel).
The VOLTAGE DROP refers to the percent of voltage lost due to resistance.
All distances calculated in feet for copper wire.

State Energy Offices

The ~ symbol denotes a state that allows net metering (as of early 2005). In addition, the states of Florida, Illinois, Michigan, Idaho, and Arizona have some utilities that support net metering without a state-wide law.

Alabama Energy Office
Dept. of Economic and
    Community Affairs
401 Adams Avenue
P.O. Box 5690
Montgomery, AL 36103-5690
Phone: (334) 242-5292
Fax: (334) 242-0552
www.adeca.alabama.gov

Alaska Energy Authority
Alaska Industrial Development
    and Export Authority
813 W. Northern Lights Blvd.
Anchorage, AK 9950
Phone: (907) 269-4625
Fax: (907) 269-3044
www.aidea.org/aea.htm

Arizona Energy Office
Arizona Dept. of Commerce
1700 W. Washington, Suite 220
Phoenix, AZ 85007
Phone: (602) 771-1100
Fax: (602) 771-1203
www.azcommerce.com/Energy/

~Arkansas Energy Office
Arkansas Industrial Development
    Commission
One Capitol Mall
Little Rock, AR 72201
Phone: (501) 682-7377
Fax: (501) 682-2703
www.1800arkansas.com/Energy/

**~California Energy
    Commission**
1516 Ninth Street, MS #32
Sacramento, CA 95814
Phone: (916) 654-4287
Fax: (916) 654-4420
www.energy.ca.gov

~ Colorado Energy Office
Governor's Office of Energy
    Management / Conservation
225 East 16th Avenue, Suite 650
Denver, CO 80203
Phone: (303) 894-2383
Fax: (303) 894-2388
www.state.co.us/oemc

~Connecticut Energy Office
Connecticut Office of Policy and
    Management
450 Capitol Ave MS#52Enr
PO Box 341441
Hartford, CT 06134-1441
Phone: (860) 418-6374
Fax: (860) 418-6495
www.opm.state.ct.us

~ Delaware Energy Office
Department of Natural Resources
    and Environmental Control
146 South Governors Avenue
Dover, DE 19901
Phone: (302) 739-1530
Fax: (302) 739-1527
www.delaware-energy.com

**~District of Columbia Energy
    Office**
2000 14th Street NW, Suite 300E
Washington, DC 20009
Phone: (202) 673-6718
Fax: (202) 673-6725
www.dcenergy.org

Florida Energy Office
Florida Dept. of Environmental
    Protection
3800 Commonwealth Blvd. MS-19
Tallahassee, FL 32399-3000
Phone: (850) 245-2940
Fax: (850) 245-2947
www.dep.state.fl.us/energy/

**~Georgia Division of Energy
    Resources**
Georgia Environmental Facilities
    Authority
100 Peachtree Street NW
Suite 2090
Atlanta, GA 30303-1911
Phone: (404) 656-5176
Fax: (404) 656-7970
www.gefa.org/energy_program.html

~ Hawaii Energy Office
Energy Resources and Technology
   Division
235 S. Beretania St., Room 502
P.O. Box 2359
Honolulu, Hawaii 96804-2359
Phone: (808) 587-3807
Fax: (808) 586-2536
www.hawaii.gov/dbedt/ert/energy

Idaho Energy Division
Idaho Dept. of Water Resources
1301 N. Orchard Street
Boise, Idaho 83706
Phone: (208) 327-7900
Fax: (208) 327-7866
www.idwr.state.id.us/energy

Illinois Energy Bureau
Illinois Dept. of Commerce and
   Economic Opportunity
620 East Adams
Springfield, IL 62701
Phone: (217) 782-7500
Fax: (217) 785-2618
*www.illinoisbiz.biz/ho_recycling_*
   energy.html

~ Indiana Energy Office
Department of Commerce
One North Capitol, Suite 700
Indianapolis, IN 46204-2288
Phone: (317) 232-8939
Fax: (317) 232-8995
www.state.in.us/doc/energy

~ Iowa Energy Bureau
Iowa Dept. of Natural Resources
Wallace State Office Building
East 9th & Grand Avenue
Des Moines, IA 50319
Phone: (515) 281-8681
Fax: (515) 281-6794
www.state.ia.us/dnr/energy

Kansas Energy Programs
Kansas Corporation Commission
1500 SW Arrowhead Road
Topeka, Kansas 66604-4027
Phone: (785) 271-3349
Fax: (785) 271-3268
www.kcc.state.ks.us/energy/index.
   html

~ Kentucky Division of Energy
663 Teton Trail
Frankfort, KY 40601
Phone: (502) 564-7192
Fax: (502) 564-7484
www.energy.ky.gov

Louisiana Energy Office
Technology Assessment Division
   Dept. of Natural Resources
P.O. Box 44156
617 North Third Street
Baton Rouge, LA 70802
Phone: (225) 342-1399
Fax: (225) 342-1397
www.dnr.state.la.us

~ Maine Division of Energy
   Programs
Maine Public Utilities
   Commission
State House Station No. 18
Augusta, ME 04333-0018
Phone: (207) 624-7495
Fax: (207) 287-8461
http://bundlemeup.org/

~ Maryland Energy Office
Maryland Energy Administration
1623 Forest Drive, Suite 300
Annapolis, MD 21403
Phone: (410) 260-7511
Fax: (410) 974-2875
www.energy.state.md.us

~ Massachusetts Division of
   Energy Resources
Dept. of Economic Development
100 Cambridge Street, Suite 1020
   Boston, MA 02114
Phone: (617) 727-4732
Fax: (617) 727-0030
www.magnet.state.ma.us/doer

Michigan Energy Office
Michigan Dept. of Consumer
   and Industry Services
P.O. Box 30221
Lansing, MI 48909
Phone: (517) 241-6180
Fax: (517) 241-6101
www.michigan.gov/mpsc

~ Minnesota Energy Division
Minnesota Dept. of Commerce
85 7th Place East, Suite 500
St. Paul, MN 55101-2198
Phone: (651) 297-2545
Fax: (651) 282-2568
www.commerce.state.mn.us

Mississippi Energy Division
MS Development Authority
P.O. Box 850
510 George Street, Suite 300
Jackson, MS 39205-0850
Phone: (601) 359-6600
Fax: (601) 359-6642
www.mississippi.org/programs/energy
   _renew_alt_energy.htm

Missouri Energy Center
Dept. of Natural Resources
P.O. Box 176
169A E. Elm Street
Jefferson City, MO 65102
Phone: (573) 751-4000
Fax: (573) 751-6860
www.dnr.state.mo.us/energy

~ Montana Energy Office
Dept. of Environmental Quality
P.O. Box 200901
1100 North Last Chance Gulch
    Room 401-H
Helena, MT 59620-0901
Phone: (406) 841-5240
Fax: (406) 841-5222
www.deq.state.mt.us/energy/

Nebraska Energy Office
State Capitol Building, 9th Floor
P.O. Box 95085
1111 "O" Street, Suite 223
Lincoln, NE 68509-5085
Phone: (402) 471-2867
Fax: (402) 471-3064
www.nol.org/home/NEO/

~ Nevada Energy Office
Dept. of Business and Industry
727 Fairview Drive, Suite F
Carson City, NV 89701
Phone: (775) 687-5975
Fax: (775) 687-4914
http://energy.state.nv.us

~ New Hampshire Energy Office
Governor's Office of Energy &
    Community Services
57 Regional Drive
Concord, NH 03301
Phone: (603) 271-2155
Fax: (603) 271-2615
www.nh.gov/oep

**~ New Jersey Office of
    Clean Energy**
NJ Board of Public Utilities
Two Gateway Center
Trenton, NJ 07102
Phone: (609) 777-3335
Fax: (609) 777-3330
www.bpu.state.nj.us

~ New Mexico Energy Office
New Mexico Energy, Minerals
    and Natural Resources Dept.
1220 S. St. Francis Drive
P.O. Box 6429
Santa Fe, NM 87505
Phone: (505) 476-3310
Fax: (505) 476-3322
www.emnrd.state.nm.us/ecmd/

**~ New York State Energy
    Research and Development
    Authority**
17 Columbia Circle
Albany, NY 12203
Phone: (866) NYSERDA
Fax: (518) 862-1091
www.nyserda.org

North Carolina Energy Office
NC Dept. of Administration
1340 Mail Service Center
Raleigh, NC 27699
Phone: (919) 733-2230
Fax: (919) 733-2953
www.energync.net

~ North Dakota Energy Office
Division of Community Services
North Dakota Dept. of Commerce
P.O. Box 2057
1600 E. Century Avenue, Suite 2
Bismarck, ND 58502-2057
Phone: (701) 328-5300
Fax: (701) 328-2308
www.state.nd.us/dcs/Energy

**~ Ohio Office of Energy
    Efficiency**
Ohio Dept. of Development
77 South High Street, 26th Floor
P.O. Box 1001
Columbus, OH 43216-1001
Phone: (614) 466-6797
Fax: (614) 466-1864
www.odod.state.oh.us/cdd/oee/

~ Oklahoma Energy Office
Oklahoma Dept. of Commerce
P.O. Box 26980
6601 North Broadway
Oklahoma City, OK 73126
Phone: (405) 815-6552
Fax: (405) 815-5344
www.okcommerce.gov/

~ Oregon Energy Office
625 Marion Street, N.E.
Salem, OR 97310
Phone: (503) 378-4040
Fax: (503) 373-7806
http://egov.oregon.gov/ENERGY/

~ Pennsylvania Energy Office
Department of Environmental
    Protection
P.O. Box 2063
400 Market Street, RCSOB
Harrisburg, PA 17105
Phone: (717) 783-0542
Fax: (717) 783-2703
www.dep.state.pa.us/

~ Rhode Island Energy Office
One Capital Hill, 2nd Floor
Providence, RI 02908
Phone: (401) 222-3370
Fax: (401) 222-1260
www.riseo.state.ri.us/

South Carolina Energy Office
1201 Main Street, Suite 600
Columbia, SC 29201
Phone: (803) 737-8030
Fax: (803) 737-9846
www.state.sc.us/energy/

South Dakota Energy Office
Governor's Office of Economic
  Development
711 E. Wells Avenue
Pierre, SD 57501-3369
Phone: (605) 773-5032
Fax: (605) 773-3256
www.sdgreatprofits.com/

Tennessee Energy Division
Department of Economics &
  Community Development
312 8th Avenue N, 9th Floor
Nashville, Tennessee 37243
Phone: (615) 741-2994
Fax: (615) 741-5070
www.state.tn.us/ecd/energy.htm

~ Texas Energy Office
State Energy Conservation Office
Texas Comptroller /Public Accounts
111 E. 17th Street- 11th Floor
Austin, TX 78701
Phone: (512) 463-1931
Fax: (512) 475-2569
www.seco.cpa.state.tx.us/

~Utah Energy Office
1594 W. North Temple, Ste 3610
P.O. Box 146480
Salt Lake City, UT 84114-6480
Phone: (801) 538-5428
Fax: (801) 538-4795
www.energy.utah.gov

**~ Vermont Energy Efficiency
  Division**
Vermont Dept. of Public Service
112 State Street, Drawer 20
Montpelier, VT 05620-2601
Phone: (802) 828-2811
Fax: (802) 828-2342
*http://www.state.vt.us/psd/Menu
  /Energy_Efficiency_and_
  Renewable_Energy.htm*

~ Virginia Division of Energy
Virginia Department of Mines,
  Minerals & Energy
202 N. Ninth Street, 8th Floor
Richmond, VA 23219
Phone: (804) 692-3200
Fax: (804) 692-3238
www.mme.state.va.us/de

**~ Washington State Energy
  Program**
925 Plum Street, SE, Bldg #4
P.O. Box 43165
Olympia, WA 98504-3165
Phone: (360) 956-2000
Fax: (360) 956-2217
www.energy.wsu.edu

**West Virginia Energy
  Efficiency Program**
WV Development Office
Building 6, Room 645
State Capitol Complex
Charleston, WV 25305
Phone: (304) 558-0350
Fax: (304) 558-0362
www.wvdo.org/community/eep.html

~ Wisconsin Energy Bureau
Department of Administration
101 E. Wilson Street, 6th Floor
P.O. Box 7868
Madison, WI 53707-7868
Phone: (608) 266-8234
Fax: (608) 267-6931
www.doa.state.wi.us/energy/

~Wyoming Energy Office
Minerals, Energy & Transportation
Wyoming Business Council
214 West 15th Street
Cheyenne, WY 82002
Phone: (307) 777-2800
Fax: (307) 777-2837
*www.wyomingbusiness.org/
  minerals/*

Puerto Rico Energy Office
PO Box 9066600
Puerta de Tierra
San Juan, Puerto Rico 00906
Phone: (787) 724-8777
Fax: (787) 721-3089

Resources

These two pages list major players in the solar/wind industry. Further research on the internet will provide additional resources.

MAJOR PHOTOVOLTAIC MANUFACTURERS

Kyocera Solar
www.kyocerasolar.com

BP Solar
www.bpsolar.com

Evergreen Solar
www.evergreensolar.com

GE Solar
www.gepower.com/prod_serv/products/solar/en/index.htm

Sharp Solar Systems
http://solar.sharpusa.com

Shell Solar
http://shellsolar.com

Matrix/Photowatt Solar Technologies
www.matrixsolar.com

Mitsubishi Electric
http://global.mitsubishielectric.com/bu/solar/

UNI-SOLAR® Products
www.uni-solar.com

PV MOUNTING HARDWARE MANUFACTURERS

UniRac
www.unirac.com

Direct Power and Water
www.directpower.com

Professional Solar Products
www.prosolar.com

INVERTER MANUFACTURERS

Beacon Power
www.beaconpower.com

Fronius USA Solar Electronics
www.fronius.com/world-wide/usa.solarelectronics/about/index.htm

OutBack Power Systems
www.outbackpower.com

PV Powered
www.pvpowered.com

Sharp Electronics
http://solar.sharpusa.com

SMA
www.sma-america.com

Xantrex Technology
www.xantrex.com

BATTERY MANUFACTURERS

Concorde Battery Corporation
www.concordebattery.com

Hawker Batteries
www.hawkerpowersource.com

MK Battery
www.mkbattery.com

WIND RESOURCES

African Wind Power
www.abundantre.com

Bergey Wind Power
www.bergey.com

Proven Wind Turbines
www.solarwindworks.com

Southwest Windpower Inc.
www.windenergy.com

Wind Turbine Industries Corp.
www.windturbine.net

OTHER COMPANIES NOTED IN THIS BOOK

Affinity Energy
www.affinityenergy.com

Blue Sky Energy, Inc.
www.blueskyenergyinc.com

DC Power Systems
www.dcpower-systems.com

Fat Spaniel
www.fatspaniel.com

Right Hand Engineering
www.righthandeng.com

Gloal Resource Options
www.globalresourceoptions.com

Real Goods
www.realgoods.com

Summit Electrical Service
www.summit-e.com

Sunlight Solar Energy
www.sunlightsolar.com

Triangle Electrical Systems
www.trianglesystems.com

EDUCATION & CLASSES

Institute for Solar Living
www.solarliving.org

Midwest Renewable Energy Association
www.the-mrea.org

Solar Energy International
www.solarenergy.org

ORGANIZATIONS

American Solar Energy Society
www.ases.org
Check here for your local chapter

American Wind Energy Assn.
www.awea.org

Center for Renewable Energy & Sustainable Technology www.crest.org

International Solar Energy Society
www.ises.org

Interstate Renewable Energy Council
www.irecusa.org

North American Board of Certified Energy Practitioners (NABCEP)
www.nabcep.org

Solar Energy Industries Assn.
www.seia.org

REFERENCE WEB SITES

Contractors License Reference Site
www.contractors-license.org

Database of State Incentives for Renewable Energy
www.dsireusa.org

Energy Star (*energy ratings*)
www.energystar.gov

Renewable Energy Access
www.renewableenergyaccess.com

SolarAccess
www.solaraccess.com

SolarBuzz
www.solarbuzz.com

U.S. Department of Energy's EERE (Energy Efficiency and Renewable Energy)
www.eere.energy.gov

U.S. Solar Radiation Maps
http://rredc.nrel.gov/solar/ old_data/nsrdb/redbook/atlas

Wind Energy Maps/Tables
http://rredc.nrel.gov/wind/ pubs/atlas/maps.html

http://rredc.nrel.gov/wind/ pubs/atlas/tables.html

MAGAZINES

BackHome **Magazine**
www.backhomemagazine.com

Home Power
www.homepower.com

Mother Earth News
www.motherearthnews.com

Solar Today
www.solartoday.org

More Books and Reference Reading

Architectural Resource Guide; Northern California Architects/Designers/Planners for Social Responsibility. Where to find all those recycled, sustainable, or better building materials, and what to do with them.

Buying a Photovoltaic Solar Electric System, A Consumer Guide, 2003 Edition; California Energy Commission. *www.energy.ca.gov/reports/2003-03-11_500-03-014F.PDF*

Consumer Guide to Home Energy Savings, 8th Edition; American Council for an Energy Efficient Economy. An abundance of tips & proven advice with lists of top energy-efficient appliances.

A Guide to Photovoltaic (PV) System Design and Installation; Endecon Engineering and Regional Economic Research for the California Energy Commission. This guide (PDF file) to properly installing grid-tie systems has been the model for many California installers. *www.energy.ca.gov/reports/2001-09-04_500-01-020.PDF*

Natural Home Heating: The Complete Guide to Renewable Energy Options by Greg Pahl; Chelsea Green Publishing. A well-organized tour of renewable home-heating options, including wood, pellet, corn and grain-fired stoves, fireplaces, furnaces, boilers, masonry heaters, active and passive solar systems, and heat pumps.

The New Ecological Home by Dan Chiras; Chelsea Green Publishing. How to minimize the ecological impact of new construction.

The Not So Big House by Sarah Susanka; Taunton Press. Housing that's a treat to senses and spirit while protecting your pocketbook.

Photovoltaics: Design and Installation Manual, Solar Energy International. The most complete and up-to-date PV book available for pros or seriously interested homeowners.

Photovoltaic Power Systems and the National Electrical Code: Suggested Practices; J. Wiles, Southwest Technology Development Institute. A plain-english explanation of PV-related electric code. Updated and republished periodically.

Power with Nature: Solar and Wind Energy Demystified by Rex Ewing; PixyJack Press. More in-depth study of off-grid renewable energy.

The Solar House: Passive Heating and Cooling by Dan Chiras; Chelsea Green Publishing. An up-to-date primer on regional passive solar design—the only intelligent way to build a house.

Solar Living Sourcebook, **12th edition**; Real Goods. The definitive retail guide to renewable energy. Part textbook, part catalog. Also contains J. Wiles Suggested Practices (listed above).

Wind Energy Basics by Paul Gipe; Chelsea Green Publishing. A guide to small and micro wind systems. All the experience, advice, and resources of Paul's complete book (*Wind Power: Renewable Energy for Home, Farm and Business*), but without the big commercial and industrial turbines.

Glossary

Absorption Stage A stage of the battery-charging process performed by the charge controller, where the batteries are held at the bulk-charging voltage for a specified time period, usually one hour.

Alternating Current (AC) Electric current that reverses its direction of flow at regular intervals, usually many times per second; common household current is AC.

Alternative Energy Energy that is not popularly used and is usually environmentally sound, such as solar or wind energy, hydrogen fuel, or biodiesel. *See also* Renewable Energy.

Amorphous Solar Cell Type of solar cell constructed by using several thin layers of molten silicon. Amorphous solar cells cost less to produce and perform better in sub-optimal lighting conditions, but need more surface area than conventional crystalline cells to produce an equal amount of power.

Ampere (Amp) Unit of electrical current, thus the rate of electron flow. One volt across one ohm of resistance is equal to a current flow of one ampere.

Ampere Hour (AH) A current of one ampere flowing for one hour. Used primarily to rate battery capacity and solar or wind output.

Array *See* Photovoltaic Array.

Battery Electrochemical cells enclosed within a single container and electrically interconnected in a series / parallel arrangement designed to provide a specific DC operating voltage and current level. Batteries for PV systems are commonly 6- or 12-volts, and are used in 12, 24 or 48-volt operations.

Battery Cell The basic functional unit in a storage battery. It consists of one or more positive electrodes or plates, an electrolyte that permits the passage of charged ions, one or more negative electrodes or plates, and the separators between plates of opposite polarity.

Battery Capacity Total amount of electrical current, expressed in ampere-hours (AH), that a battery can deliver to a load under a specific set of conditions.

Battery Life Period during which a battery is capable of operating at or above its specified capacity or efficiency level. A battery's useful life is generally considered to be over when a fully charged cell can only deliver 80 percent of its rated capacity. Beyond this point, the battery capacity diminishes rapidly. Life may be measured in cycles and/or years, depending on the type of service for which the battery was designed.

Blocking Diode A semiconductor connected in series with a solar module or array, used to prevent the reverse flow of electricity from the battery bank back into the array, when there is little or no solar output.

Think of it as a one-way valve that allows electrons to flow forward, but not backward.

Building-integrated PV (BIPV) Where PV is integrated into a building, replacing conventional materials, such a siding, shingles or roofing panels.

Bulk Stage Initial stage of battery charging, where the charge controller allows maximum charging in order to reach the bulk voltage setting.

Cell *See* Photovoltaic Cell.

Cell Efficiency Percentage of electrical energy that a solar cell produces (under optimal conditions) divided by the total amount of solar energy falling on the cell. Typical efficiency for commercial cells is in the range of 12 to 15 percent.

Charge Controller Component located in the circuit between the solar array or wind turbine, and the battery bank. Its job is to bring the batteries to an optimal state of charge, without overcharging them. Most charge controllers have digital displays to help monitor system status and performance. MPPT charge controllers go a step further, by converting excess array voltage into usable amperage.

Circuit A system of conductors connected together for the purpose of carrying an electric current from a generating source, through the devices that use the electricity (the loads), and back to the source.

Circuit Breaker Safety device that shuts off power (i.e. it creates an open circuit) when it senses too much current.

Conductor A material—usually a metal, such as copper—that facilitates the flow of electrons.

Conversion Efficiency *See* Cell Efficiency.

Current Flow of electricity between two points. Measured in amps.

Depth of Discharge (DOD) The ampere-hours removed from a fully charged battery, expressed as a percentage of rated capacity. For example, the removal of 25 ampere-hours from a fully charged 100 ampere-hour rated battery results in a 25-percent depth of discharge. For optimum health in most batteries, the DOD should never exceed 50 percent.

Direct Current (DC) Electrical current that flows in only one direction. It is the type of current produced by solar cells, and the only current that can be stored in a battery.

Distributed System A system installed near where the electricity is used, as opposed to a central system—such as a coal or nuclear power plant—that supplies electricity to the electrical grid. A grid-tied residential solar system is a distributed system.

Electrical Grid A large distribution network—including towers, poles, and transmission lines—that delivers electricity over a wide area.

Electric Circuit *See* Circuit.

Electric Current *See* Current.

Electricity In a practical sense, the controlled flow of electrons through a conductor. In a scientific sense, the non-gravitational and non-nuclear repulsive and attractive forces governing much of the behavior of charged subatomic particles.

Electrode A conductor used to lead current into or out of a nonmetallic part of a circuit, such as a battery's positive and negative electrodes.

Electrolyte Fluid used in batteries as the transport medium for positively and negatively charged ions. In lead-acid batteries this is a somewhat diluted sulfuric acid.

Electron Negatively-charged particle. An electrical current is a stream of electrons moving through an electrical conductor.

Energy The capacity for performing work. A ball resting on the top of a hill is said to have potential energy, while the same ball rolling down the hill is imbued with kinetic energy. Solar cells convert electromagnetic energy (light) from the sun into electrical energy, while wind turbines convert the kinetic energy of the air into first mechanical energy, and then electrical energy.

Energy Audit An inspection process that determines how much energy you use in your home, usually accompanied by specific suggestions for saving energy.

Equalization A controlled process of overcharging non-sealed lead-acid batteries, intended to clean lead sulfates

from the battery's plates, and restore all cells to an equal state-of-charge.

Float Stage A battery-charging operation performed by the charge controller in which enough energy is supplied to meet all loads, plus internal component losses, thus always keeping the battery up to full power and ready for service. Float voltage is somewhat lower than bulk voltage.

Fossil Fuels Carbon- and hydrogen-laden fuels formed underground from the remains of long-dead plants and animals. Crude oil, natural gas and coal are fossil fuels.

Full Sun Scientific definition of solar power density received at the surface of the earth at noon on a clear day. Defined as 1,000 watts per square meter (W/m^2). Reality varies from 600 to 1,200 W/m^2, depending on latitude, altitude, and atmospheric purity.

Greenhouse Effect A warming effect that occurs when heat from the sun becomes trapped in the Earth's atmosphere due to the heat-absorbing properties of certain (greenhouse) gases.

Greenhouse Gases Gases responsible for trapping heat from the sun within the Earth's atmosphere. Water vapor and carbon dioxide are the most prevalent, but methane, ozone, chlorofluorocarbons and nitrogen oxides are also important greenhouse gases.

Grid *See* Electrical Grid.

Grid-Connected PV System A solar PV system that is tied into the utility's electrical grid. When generating more power than necessary to power all its loads, the system sends the surplus to the grid. At night, the system draws power from the grid.

Hertz (Hz) A unit denoting the frequency of an electromagnetic wave, equal to one cycle per second. In alternating current, the frequency at which the current switches direction. In the U.S. this is usually 60 cycles per second (60 Hz).

Hybrid System Power-generating system consisting of two or more subsystems, such as a wind turbine or diesel generator, and a photovoltaic system.

Insolation Measure of the amount of solar radiation reaching the surface of the

Earth. According to NREL, "this term has been generally replaced by solar irradiance because of the confusion of the word with insulation." *See* Irradiance.

Inverter Component that transforms the direct current (DC) flowing from a solar system or battery to alternating current (AC) for use in the home. Also called a power inverter.

Irradiance Rate at which radiant energy arrives at a specific area of the Earth's surface during a specific time interval. Measured in W/m^2.

I-V Curve A graph that plots the current versus the voltage from a solar cell, as the electrical load (or resistance) is increased from short circuit (no load) to open circuit (maximum voltage). The shape of the curve characterizes the cell's performance. Three important points on the I-V curve are the open-circuit voltage, short-circuit current, and peak or maximum power (operating) point.

Junction Box (J-Box) Enclosure on the back of a solar module where it is connected (wired) to other solar modules.

Kilowatt (kW) Unit of electrical power, equal to one thousand watts.

Kilowatt-Hour (kWh) One thousand watts being used over a period of one hour. The kWh is the usual billing unit of energy for utility companies.

Life-Cycle Cost Estimated cost of owning, operating, and disposing of a system over its useful life.

Load Anything that draws power from an electrical circuit.

Maximum Power Point Tracking (MPPT) Technology used by direct grid-tied inverters and some charge controllers to convert, through the use of DC-DC power converters, excess array voltage into usable amperage, by tracking the optimal power point of the I-V curve.

Megawatt (MW) One million watts; 1,000 kilowatts. Commercial power plants and wind farms are usually rated in megawatts.

Module *See* photovoltaic module.

Monocrystalline Solar Cell Type of solar cell made from a thin slice of a single large sil-

icon crystal. Also known as single-crystal solar cell.

Multicrystalline Solar Cell *See* polycrystalline solar cell.

National Electrical Code (NEC) The U.S. minimum inspection requirements for all types of electrical installations, including solar/wind systems.

NEMA (National Electrical Manufacturers Association) The U.S. trade organization which sets standards for the electrical manufacturing industry.

NREL (National Renewable Energy Laboratory) Based in Golden, Colorado, NREL is the principal research laboratory for the DOE Office of Energy Efficiency and Renewable Energy. Operated by Midwest Research Institute and Battelle, NREL concentrates on studying, testing and developing renewable energy technologies.

Net Metering A practice used in conjunction with a solar- or wind-electric system. The electric utility's meter tracks the home's net power usage, spinning forward when electricity is drawn from the utility, and spinning backward when the solar or wind system is generating more electricity than is currently needed to run the home's loads.

Ohm Measure of the resistance to current flow in electrical circuits, equal to the amount of resistance overcome by one volt in causing one ampere to flow.

Orientation Term used to describe the direction that a solar module or array faces. The two components of orientation are the tilt angle (the number of degrees the panel is raised from the horizontal position) and the aspect angle, (the degree by which the panel deviates from facing due south).

Panel *See* Solar Panel.

Parallel Connection Wiring configuration whereby the current is given more than one path to follow, thus amperage is increased while voltage remains unchanged. In DC systems, parallel wiring is positive to positive (+ to +) and negative to negative (- to -). *See also* Series Connection.

Passive Solar Home Home designed to use sunlight for direct heating and lighting, without circulating pumps or energy conversion systems. This is achieved through the use of energy efficient materials (such as windows, skylights and Trombe walls) and proper design and orientation of the home.

Peak Load Maximum amount of electricity being used at any one point during the day.

Photon Basic unit of light. A photon can act as either a particle or a wave, depending on how it's activity is measured. The shorter the wavelength of a stream of photons, the more energy it possesses. This is why ultraviolet (UV) light is so destructive, while infrared (IR) is not.

Photovoltaic (PV) Refers to the technology of converting sunlight directly into electricity, through the use of photovoltaic (solar) cells.

Photovoltaic Array A system of interconnected PV modules (solar panels) acting together to produce a single electrical output.

Photovoltaic Cell The basic unit of a PV (solar) module. Crystalline photovoltaic cells produce an electrical potential of around 0.5 volts. The higher voltages typical in PV modules are achieved by connecting solar cells together in series.

Photovoltaic Module Collection of solar cells joined as a unit within a single frame. Commonly called a "solar panel."

Photovoltaic System Complete set of interconnected components—including a solar array, inverter, etc.—designed to convert sunlight into usable electricity.

Polycrystalline Solar Cell Type of solar cell made from many small silicon crystals (crystallites). Because of the numerous grain boundaries, devices that employ this design will operate with slightly reduced efficiency. Also known as a polycrystalline solar cell.

PV Photovoltaic.

Rated Power Nominal power output of an inverter; some units cannot produce rated power continuously.

Renewable Energy (RE) Energy obtained from sources that are essentially inexhaustible (unlike, for example, fossil fuels, of which there is a finite supply). Renewable sources of energy include conventional hydroelectric power, wood, waste, geothermal, wind, photovoltaic, and solar-thermal energy.

Semiconductor Material that has an electrical conductivity in between that of a metal and an insulator. Typical semiconductors for PV cells include silicon, gallium arsenide, copper indium diselenide, and cadmium telluride.

Series Connection A wiring configuration where the current is given but one path to follow, thus increasing voltage without changing the amperage. Series wiring is positive to negative (+ to -) or negative to positive (- to +). *See also* Parallel Connection.

Silicon (Si) The most common semiconductor material used in the manufacture of PV cells. In the periodic table, it is element number 14, positioned between aluminum and phosphorus.

Single-Crystal Silicon *See* Monocrystalline Solar Cell.

Solar Cell *See* Photovoltaic Cell.

Solar Energy Energy from the sun. Virtually all energy on Earth—including solar, wind, hydroelectric and even fossil-fuel energy—originated as solar energy.

Solar Insolation *See* Irradiance.

Solar Module *See* Photovoltaic Module.

Solar Panel Common term used to describe a PV (solar) module. "Solar panel" refers to both photovoltaic modules, used for making electricity, and solar hot-water panels, used to augment a home's heating system.

Solar Power *See* Solar Energy.

Stand-Alone A solar-electric system that operates without connection to the utility grid, or another supply of electricity. Typically, unused daylight energy production is stored in a battery bank to provide power at night. Stand-alone systems are used primarily in remote locations, such as mountain areas, ocean platforms or communication towers.

Thin Film *See* Amorphous Solar Cell.

Tilt Angle The angle of inclination of a module measured from the horizontal. The most productive tilt angle is one in which the surface of the module is exactly perpendicular to sun's rays.

Volt (V) A unit of electrical force, analogous to the water pressure within a garden hose. It is equal to the amount of electromotive force that will cause a steady current of one ampere to flow through a resistance of one ohm.

Watt (W) Unit of electrical power used to indicate the rate of energy produced or consumed by an electrical device. One ampere of current flowing at a potential of one volt produces one watt of power. Wind turbines and PV modules are often rated in watts.

Watt-hour (Wh) Unit of energy equal to one watt of power being used or produced for one hour.

Wind Energy The kinetic energy present in wind, measured in watts per square meter (W/m^2). Wind turbines convert the kinetic energy into mechanical energy through the use of propeller blades, which in turn drive an alternator to produce electricity.

Index

Where Do We Get Our Energy?

Coal
22.31 quads

Imports
31.02 quads

Natural Gas
19.64 quads

Crude Oil
12.15 quads

Renewable Energy
6.15 quads

Nuclear Electric Power
7.97 quads

Natural Gas Plant Liquids
2.343 quads

2003 U.S. Energy Sources
Numbers listed in Quadrillion Btu.
Source: DOE / EIA

How Does The Energy Get Used?

Transportation
26.9 quads

Residential
21.2 quads

Commercial
17.5 quads

Industrial
32.5 quads

2003 U.S. Energy Consumption
Numbers listed in Quadrillion Btu.
Source: DOE / EIA

Meet the Authors

W hat do a Colorado conservative and California liberal have in common? For these two authors, they share an enthusiasm for renewable energy, and the belief that it can work for anyone who decides to be a part of the energy solution. Whether you embrace solar and wind energy for environmental reasons, think it's a great way to cut your utility bills, or simply want independence from power-grid failures, you will find that renewable energy goes beyond politics and is an incredibly smart move toward a secure future.

Rex Ewing has lived blissfully off-grid with solar and wind energy since 1999 when he left the dusty plains of Colorado and headed for the Rockies to build his wife, LaVonne, a long-promised log home. When he's not writing books or magazine articles about renewable energy—or his first love, horses—he and LaVonne are probably trekking through the back country, canoeing, or enjoying the 50-mile view from their deck.

Before moving to the mountains to concentrate on his writing, Ewing raised grass hay and high-strung Thoroughbred race horses in the Platte River valley. Whenever his employees were clever enough to corral him behind a desk, he served as CEO of a well-respected equine nutrition firm, where he formulated and marketed a successful line of equine supplements worldwide.

Doug Pratt grew up in a wonderful rural community of Frank Lloyd Wright homes, but after 23 Michigan winters, he figured it wasn't going to get any better and ran off to northern California to be a good hippie and enjoy milder winters. Within a year the Arab Oil Embargo hit, which ignited a lifelong interest in renewable energy and energy conservation. He has lived in passive solar homes, on and off-grid since 1980, and worked in the RE industry as a technician, consultant, teacher, and writer since 1985. His house has been solar grid-tied since 2000 and his Toyota Prius was the first one sold into Mendocino County. And because the scenery is so beautiful, the roads so swoopy, and the climate so friendly in northern coastal California, his favorite recreation is two-up day trips on his BMW motorcycle.

Other alternative energy titles from **PixyJack Press, LLC**

Power With Nature
Solar and Wind Energy Demystified

REX A. EWING

Is alternative energy for you? Learn how to capture energy from the sun, wind and water to create electricity for home. Focuses on off-grid homes but includes a chapter on utility grid-tie options. Also discussed: solar hot water, home heating and water pumping options. Written in plain English by someone who has lived with solar and wind energy since 1999.

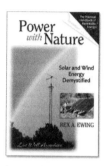

HYDROGEN—Hot Stuff Cool Science
Journey to a world of hydrogen energy and fuels cells at the Wasserstoff Farm

REX A. EWING

Science is explained, ideas illuminated and myths dispelled in this highly readable book about what many experts are calling the most important new energy for planet Earth. Learn where hydrogen comes from, how it will be stored and then used to power our cars, make backup electricity for homes and buildings, and much more. Discover how fuel cells work, and read about global warming and the role of hydrogen in our future. And be prepared to have more fun discovering science and technology than you thought possible.

Logs, Wind and Sun
Handcraft your own log home...then power it with nature

REX A. EWING AND LAVONNE EWING

An inspiring, hands-on guide to self-sufficiency takes you through every step of handcrafting your own log home and then bringing it to life with power from the wind and sun. Drawing on their own experiences, and those of others in the Colorado Rockies, they show you—simply and enjoyably—just how attainable your dream of off-the-grid, log home living can be.

A solar and wind-powered independent publisher

PixyJack Press LLC

To order autographed copies:
PO Box 149 • Masonville, CO 80541
www.PixyJackPress.com